YOUR
EXECUTIVE
IMAGE

YOUR EXECUTIVE IMAGE

HOW TO LOOK YOUR BEST & PROJECT SUCCESS FOR MEN AND WOMEN

VICTORIA A. SEITZ

ADAMS MEDIA CORPORATION
HOLBROOK, MASSACHUSETTS

Published by
Adams Media Corporation
260 Center Street, Holbrook, MA 02343

ISBN: 1-58062-178-3

Printed in Canada.

J I H G F E D C B

Library of Congress Cataloging-in-Publication Data
Seitz, Victoria A.
Your executive image / by Vicoria A. Seitz.--2nd ed.
p.   cm.
Includes bibliographical references and index.
ISBN 1-58062-178-3
1. Executives. 2. Self-presentation. 3. Identity (Psychology)
4. Clothing and dress. 5. Interpersonal communication. I. Title.
HD38.2 .S45   2000
658.4'09--dc21   99-053182

This publication is designed to provide accurate and authoritative information with regard to the subject matter covered. It is sold with the understanding that the publisher is not engaged in rendering legal, accounting, or other professional advice. If legal advice or other expert assistance is required, the services of a competent professional person should be sought.
— From a *Declaration of Principles* jointly adopted by a Committee of the American Bar Association and a Committee of Publishers and Associations

Cover photo by H.G. Rossi

This book is available at quantity discounts for bulk purchases.
For information, call 1-800-872-5627.

Visit our exciting small business Web site at businesstown.com

This book is dedicated to my mother,
the late Betty Merrill Seitz,
the original clotheshorse and
the epitome of style.

Table of Contents

Acknowledgments

I'd like to thank a lot of people for helping me with this project. First, my family, for giving me the support, encouragement, and drive to do this project. Thanks especially to my dad, who had more foresight than I and who gave me the idea first to write a column, then to offer seminars, and finally to write this book. I'd like to thank my dear friend Don Anderson and the 6 a.m. workout group: Sue, Lynn, Katie, Grace, Dick, Jerry, Staley, and Doryce, for being great friends and believing in me. Thanks to my agent for inspiring deadlines to start and to finish the book, and to Martin Birnbach for what he didn't realize he did—that push to get me going on this project. Thanks to Don Moore, Russell Newmans; Bob Bowler, JC Penney; and Curran Dandurran, Mary Kay Cosmetics, for endorsing the project. And to all the companies and many associations that helped me develop this material—thanks to all of you!

Preface

The image you present to others is much more than just how you look. It's your whole persona: not just the way you dress but your body language and etiquette as well. The prescriptions for success prevalent in the eighties focused on dress alone, but that, it turned out, was just the beginning. As we later found, projecting the executive image includes a command of the social graces, since so much of the business we do is conducted outside the office. As for body language—ask yourself whether you move like an executive, or whether your body is sending conflicting messages about your abilities to the people who count.

This book is designed for the nineties and beyond. It shows you how to develop your own executive style. Formerly, the ticket to success meant following strict prescriptions in dress and behavior, and the result, often, was a set of boring rituals. Creating your own look within the confines of what is appropriate for your profession and company communicates self-confidence and creativity—essential attributes in today's business environments.

After studying fashion, working in retail, and conducting numerous seminars I have found that you can dress some people up—but you can't take them out of the picture. "Dressing for success" has been somewhat useful for those who already possessed the necessary poise and social etiquette, but today, few are lucky enough to have had this training. Without it, however, your career may be severely jeopardized.

This book is the result of years of study in body language, dress, and etiquette. My father was in the military, and proper etiquette (they called it "protocol") was a part of everyday life. My parents threw a great many parties, which gave my brother and me ample opportunity to learn how to dress and act appropriately in a social setting. In this way we became socially astute at an early age. I would not trade those experiences today, much as I dreaded getting dressed up and "being sociable" at the time.

This book is designed not only to make you look good, but also to increase your confidence as you face a variety of situations. It will help enhance your presence among clients and colleagues and show you how to be socially astute. Nowadays, a lot of deals are made over lunch or dinner. If you are unfamiliar with the protocol of fine dining, you may well find yourself preoccupied with what fork to use instead of with making the deal click.

This book will also help you to read the signals given nonverbally, through our bodies. In sales, reading body language gives you a definite edge, alerting you when or when not to close, letting you know whether you're wasting your time and energy with someone who's not going to buy. Body language holds valuable information for you.

If you are an executive or owner of a business, you need to know two things: What is your image and Who is your customer? Your image is presented in the building you build or the area you rent in, the atmosphere within the walls of your business, your advertising, the products or service packages you sell, how customers are served, and what your employees look like.

This book addresses not only corporate life but businesses requiring uniforms or certain codes of dress. In my seminars I have often been asked to address employees whose "uniform" included shorts, shirts, and athletic shoes. Dressing appropriately in such a setting involves the same principles as choosing the right suit and tie.

As you read, you will learn to apply principles of design to your wardrobe, creating new designs, coordinating, and making use of optical illusion for maximum effect. These tools will enable you to create looks that are integrated—and look great on you.

Overview

"What do you want to be when you grow up?" Each of us has responded to that question at one time or another. But we should really ask, "Who do you want to be when you grow up?" Both questions must be answered as we mature, but the answers will differ. "I want to be an attorney; I want to be like the senior partner in our law firm." There are a lot of attorneys out there, each possessing individuality within the confines (if they are going to survive) of what is considered appropriate for the law profession. Who do you want to be?

Your executive image is your total persona. Mastering it is like packaging a product. Like products, each of us will be packaged differently from the next person. Expressing uniqueness in your packaging is crucially important for today's executives, as well as for up-and-coming CEO's. Why? Because such expression communicates self-confidence, creativity, and leadership.

Each of us is an individual, possessing different personalities, looks, physiques and so on. But professions also possess unique characteristics. In traditional businesses such as banking, law, and accounting, the atmosphere is conservative. Dress is restricted to pinstriped suits, dark colors, and modest styles. The atmosphere is formal and protocol prevails; dos and don'ts are black and white. Those who choose to succeed in such professions, however, will find that even they can project their individuality within the confines of their formal environments.

In marketing, sales, retailing, education, real estate, engineering, and other fields, the atmosphere is less conservative. Although choice of dress is not "anything goes," there is a greater opportunity to incorporate variety in one's wardrobe. Blazers and sport coats are commonly worn for men, while women can make use of coordinating separates and knits. Stronger colors and fashion styling can be incorporated into the professional wardrobe. The atmosphere in these professions is a bit more informal, with brainstorming sessions and roundtable discussions quite common; however, some formalities still prevail.

In the fields of public relations, art, advertising, fashion, interior design, and decoration, your key to success is inviting uniqueness in your look in order to communicate your expertise in these professions. The key to your credibility might be expressed in unique, eye-catching accessories such as a brightly colored tie, an unstructured suit, a bold neck piece, a belt, or bold-patterned fabrics. The atmosphere in these professions may be informal, and rules of conduct may be looser, but protocol is still just as important for the executive.

Before you read the chapters ahead, take time to visualize the professional you want to be. Write your own impressions on a separate sheet of paper. Think of someone you admire or aspire to be like and analyze what you think makes that person so successful. What is it about the way they dress, how they act, their mannerisms, and their body language that makes you want to be like them? Include in your analysis what makes that person unique from everyone else.

Remember, projecting the executive image is total packaging, projecting something unique but appropriate for your chosen profession. On your analysis sheet, write down your profession, the environment where you work, your position, and what you think the appropriate image is for a manager or executive in your company.

You Already Have an Image

1. Posture

2. Facial Expression and Eye Contact

3. Gestures

4. Space

5. Voice

6. Clothing Language

YOU CANNOT NOT COMMUNICATE. Even when you haven't said a word, your body has a language that communicates distinct messages to others. If what you do say conflicts with these body messages, be warned: the recipient will perceive the nonverbal communication as true. In other words, your body doesn't lie.

Body motions can be grouped into four types. The first group is referred to as *emblems*. These are widely accepted translations, such as a nod for yes and smiling as a sign for happiness.

The second group is made up of *illustrators*. These accompany verbal messages to support a point. For example, when we say the number one we might hold up one finger.

The third group consists of *regulators*. These are movements that serve, either positively or negatively, to regulate conversations. For example, to regulate a conversation positively and move it along, the parties may maintain eye contact. When someone wants to end the conversation, he or she will look down or turn his or her head or body away from the speaker.

The fourth group is that of the *adaptors*. Adaptive body motions help us to deal with feelings of uneasiness. They include nervous habits such as twisting our hair, playing with our clothing, tugging our ears, or biting our nails, habits manifested in unfamiliar or uncomfortable situations.

Is all body language universal? No. Nonverbal messages vary from culture to culture and depending on the situation. In America, the hand sign for "OK" is a circle with the thumb and index finger with the remaining fingers raised. But go to Brazil and use the same gesture, and you'll be insulting your conversational partner.

Some gestures are universal. Smiles are universally accepted as meaning happiness, while crying signals sadness.

It's important to note that when you are interpreting body language, you must read all the parts. Don't isolate someone's posture and assign meaning to it alone. Look at other gestures used and give meaning to those as well. Body language is a total package.

Moreover, impressions are meant to be broken. You might get a "wet fish" handshake and assume the person to be weak, when in reality she has arthritis. Or perhaps you come in contact with someone whose arms are folded across his chest and whose posture is bent slightly forward. If it's cold, he may be trying to stay warm; but in a warm room this projects a defensive, uninviting message. So it's important to consider the context of the signals being sent. There may be unknown reasons behind the message you receive.

In this section I will discuss the most important body parts and the messages they send. As you read, you will gain a greater sensitivity to body language and the signals others are communicating. More importantly, you will become more sensitive to the nonverbal messages *you* are communicating to others. You may be sending conflicting messages and wondering why no one seems to take you seriously at work. Perhaps you're finding it difficult to know when to close a sale on a prospective client. You may be wasting precious time with prospects who are not interested in your product or service. Knowing the body signals will enhance your abilities in your profession.

It bears repeating: In the office or at a business party, wherever you are, you're communicating. You may not be saying a word, but your eyes, gestures, posture, and the space around you speak volumes. Then again, when you do speak, how much do you distort your meaning through your tone of voice? I'm sure you've heard this at one time or another: "Don't speak to me in that tone of voice." Your tone of voice communicates much more than the words actually used. Does your tone of voice command authority and respect, or terror and mistrust?

If we cannot *not* communicate, we might as well send the right message.

ONE

Posture

Posture—the way you sit and stand—is the first crucial influence on others' first impressions of you. It says a great deal about your self-confidence, how approachable you are, and what kind of attitude you have. Posture thus plays an important role in body language.

Experts have identified "the center" as one of the most influential elements of good posture. The center is the intersection created at the midchest of the body by drawing imaginary lines from the armpits across the chest and from the midchest front to back. When someone is standing straight, his or her center is open to everyone, communicating confidence and openness. When someone is slumped over, the center is hidden, communicating a lack of enthusiasm or interest—or a lack of confidence.

When people form groups, posture projects the relationship of each individual to that group and the group's relationship with the individual. Some authorities divide group postures into categories of inclusive or noninclusive, parallel or nonparallel, and congruent or incongruent.

Let's consider the first category, inclusiveness or noninclusiveness. People form groups that exclude others by the placement of their bodies. At cocktail parties, for example, people form circles that exclude others from joining them.

The second category is parallel body orientation. When two people relate to one another, they can do so by sitting or standing either in front of each other or beside one another. When they stand next to one another, the message conveyed is one of neutrality. When they face one another, they send a signal of involvement with or reaction to the other person's topic of discussion or particular situation.

In the final category, congruence or incongruence, group members mirror or imitate one another to communicate membership in the group. When one member changes position, the others will shift positions.

Often the leader of the group or a member with higher status than the others will signal this status by taking on a different posture. This can be seen in the habits of people who have higher positions in a company, higher rank in a military organization, or greater presence in the community. Those closest to such people will eventually copy their posture to signal alliance and loyalty. Sometimes, indeed, the group leader sets the posture for the other members of the group.

What messages are conveyed in our posture? Here are some examples.

- Someone who stands tall, back straight, is generally self-confident.
- Someone who stands with curved back and lowered gaze communicates a feeling of inferiority.
- When someone leans toward you during conversation, he or she is probably involved in the conversation and interested in you.
- Conversely, when someone leans away from you during conversation, he or she is probably uninvolved.
- Relaxed posture usually indicates a favorable attitude and status.
- When both arms are folded across the chest, the person in question is generally protecting him or herself or hiding from an unfavorable situation.
- In a face-to-face situation, folding the arms across the chest usually signals disagreement.
- A partial arm barrier, such as holding on to one arm at the elbow, generally signals either a lack of self-confidence or that the person is a stranger to the group.

- Women often disguise their barriers by gripping personal objects (a purse, for example); such items are often used for protection.
- Someone who crosses his or her legs and arms while seated has most likely withdrawn from the conversation. This is also a signal used by women when they are displeased with their partner.
- A defensive or closed standing posture usually includes standing with legs and arms crossed.
- Legs uncrossed and feet placed together indicate a neutral posture.
- "Locked" ankles generally signals a defensive, closed posture or a negative emotion or attitude.
- To assume an authoritarian posture, a person may well try to make her body appear larger by putting her shoulders back, placing her hands on her hips, and facing the speaker directly.
- Placing the hands behind the back and standing slightly off-center from the speaker usually suggests a submissive attitude.
- Keeping the trunk and legs straight but turning the head away from the speaker, or supporting the head with the arm usually suggests a person's interest is fading.
- Arms and legs uncrossed communicates an open posture.
- Leaning the head and trunk to one side signals agreement.
- Crossed arms and legs indicates disagreement.

To come across as confident yet approachable, whether standing or sitting, you should appear relaxed without being sloppy, confident without being stiff. To appear approachable when dealing with lower status audiences, relax. (Relax with peers, too.) With someone of higher status than yourself, however, stand straight but not stiff.

If you are a woman selling to a man, your posture must be direct and confident. You should sit up and a bit forward in your seat. When selling to other women, however, you should be more relaxed and work more closely with the female than the male client. Your posture should also reflect respect when dealing with a woman of greater status than yourself. For men working with women, posture should be relaxed but not sloppy. Don't hide or minimize your height; stand tall and erect but not stiff or proud.

EXERCISE EXERCISE EXERCISE

EXERCISE 1

Examine your posture in the mirror. What are you communicating? Try to alter your posture for specific situations, such as when addressing someone of lower status, your peers, and someone of higher status than yourself. Become familiar with these postures so that you are aware of what your posture is communicating to others.

....
....
....
....
....

EXERCISE 2

Take a few minutes each day and simply look at other people, perhaps at the office or during lunch. What is their posture communicating about who they are? Become familiar with the different postures you see, such as selling postures and postures meant to attract the opposite sex.

....
....
....
....
....

TWO

Facial Expression and Eye Contact

The eyes have it! The face and the eyes really are the most expressive parts of our bodies. They establish rapport between people, regulate conversations or break them off. When we want to catch a waiter's attention, we do so through direct eye contact. To end a conversation, we may do the opposite—break eye contact with the other person.

The eyes have been called the "windows of the soul." Do you sometimes feel, when someone looks at you, that the person can see right through you? How many times have you found yourself thinking that you didn't trust someone because of his eyes? Shifty eyes are associated with deviousness; a lack of eye contact is associated with lying. As a matter of fact, when someone is lying, the amount of eye contact is about one-third less than when someone is telling the truth.

Actually, the eyes, in and of themselves, do not represent the most expressive parts of our body. It is how they are used and the expression of the rest of the face that give them their tremendous impact. The manipulation of the eyes and face can make or break you. (How appealing is a person who constantly squints?)

Every society has rules for eye contact and facial expressions. In the United States it's not polite to stare at another person. If someone is physically disabled or doesn't meet societal standards in one way or another, a person may look but must quickly turn away. It's dehumanizing to be stared at. Staring in our culture is often confined to observations of inanimate objects, such as art.

It's amazing how much eye contact means in our society. When a teacher wants to call on a student, heads go down immediately to avoid eye contact, which would otherwise result in being called on. When a stranger enters an elevator he or she may give brief eye contact, then shift that contact down to the floor or up towards the floor indicator. To look at anyone for any length usually indicates that we want to establish rapport with that person.

When you are walking down the street and are about to pass someone, you'll probably glance briefly at each other until you're about eight feet apart; then you'll both look away. That quick look is often followed by a glance downward to communicate that there's trust and that neither of you is afraid of the other.

The pupils of the eyes are another communicator. When someone is excited or attracted, his or her pupils dilate. When a person is angry, disenchanted with the conversation, or lying, the pupils contract. Expert poker players often look in their opponents' eyes to see whether the pupils are dilated, indicating a good hand. In business meetings, expert negotiators often look at the other person's pupils to see whether he is excited, angry or uncomfortable.

Some researchers feel that personality can be revealed by looking into someone's eyes. The larger a person's irises, for example, the more likely he will be to be emotionally expressive. Small irises generally indicate that the individual is more of a "matter of fact" person who conceals emotions. Such people, it is said, are likely to think more with their heads than with their hearts. Furthermore, they are likely to be thought of as cold-hearted and somewhat self-centered.

Eyes partially closed or squinted point to people who are channeling their thoughts. Such people have the ability to direct their attention to what they consider important. Bear in mind, though, that there might be other reasons why someone is squinting, such as glare or a case of nearsightedness.

Other parts of the face can also communicate feelings. The eyebrows often emphasize what the eyes want to say. When someone is angry, his face becomes taut, his mouth turns down at the sides, his pupils contract, his eyebrows curve towards the center of his forehead, and his forehead creases.

The combination of all these signals transmits the message in a pronounced fashion. There is no question as to the message being sent.

Your face communicates your true emotions to others. There are six basic emotions: happiness, sadness, anger, disgust, surprise, and fear. Even though you're communicating many positive words verbally, your face may be saying something else. When such a contradiction is exhibited by the person you are speaking to, go with the nonverbal communication.

In America, the business gaze is aimed directly at the eye level of the other individual, whereas a social gaze may fall below eye level but between the eyes and mouth.

The sideways glance is employed to show either interest or hostility, depending on the situation. When combined with a smile and raised eyebrows, this glance may reflect interest in another. Combined with a taut mouth and creased forehead and eyebrows, this gesture communicates hostility, suspicion, or a negative attitude overall.

The eye-block gesture is used to communicate status or boredom. This is when someone tilts her head back slightly and closes her eyes. Either she has blocked you out of the conversation or she feels superior to you.

Controlling someone's gaze is important when you want him to retain the information given in a presentation or in a face-to-face interaction. This can be done using a pen or pencil to bring the eye contact back to you. Absorption of material increases by over 50 percent when a visual aid, related to what is being said, is employed. To maintain control of the individual's gaze, try lifting a pen or pencil from the visual aid and holding it between his eyes and yours.

When giving a group presentation, eye contact with the audience is essential. If you keep yourself buried in your notes, the audience sees nothing but the top of your head. Maintain contact with your audience 75 to 85 percent of the time. Establish eye contact with the friendly faces: people who are smiling, nodding in agreement, and encouraging and supporting you and your ideas. In one-on-one conversations, you should maintain eye contact with the other person 50 to 60 percent of the time.

Your facial gestures should reflect the mood you are in or the mood you want to create. During a group presentation your expression will keep the audience alive, so vary it and keep it on the positive side. Smiles are more pleasant and less stressful on the facial muscles than frowns.

EXERCISE EXERCISE EXERCISE

EXERCISE 1

Look in the mirror and become familiar with your own facial gestures. For example, smile, look surprised, express fear and sadness. The objective of this exercise is to become sensitive to your own facial gestures and the messages you are communicating with them.

....

....

....

....

....

EXERCISE 2

Take a few minutes a day to observe other people. Watch TV and become familiar with how facial gestures support points being made and how they regulate conversation. Are facial gestures consistent with verbal messages?

....

....

....

....

....

THREE

Gestures

Gestures are vital to communicating thoughts, feelings, and ideas. They illustrate and reinforce what we want to say. They can also promote the actions or reactions you desire from your audience. Gestures can be used, together with changes in body position, to introduce a new subject matter or a new idea.

Gestures involve various parts of the body, including the head, arm, hands, face, and legs, or can involve an interaction between two or three of these body parts. As with posture and facial expressions, gestures are culturally defined.

Gestures should not be taken out of context or interpreted without consideration to other body signals. For example, hand gestures may communicate that someone wants to end the conversation, while the eyes and face are communicating otherwise.

Gestures are commonly perceived as warm or cold. Warm gestures may include leaning toward people when speaking or listening, facing them directly, smiling, touching, and gesturing expressively. Cold gestures include placing your hands on your hips, slumping, avoiding eye contact, and not smiling. Some gestures display nervousness, such as cleaning your fingernails, drumming your fingers, fiddling with objects or jewelry, looking at your watch, licking your lips, scratching your arms, and tugging your ears.

Here are some gestures and their meanings.

- Palms up commonly demonstrate openness, acceptance of an idea, and participation.
- Upturned fists can draw the listener to you as well as reinforce a point aggressively.
- Palms face down often communicate immediate authority.
- A fist with the index finger pointed to someone generally commands submission from the person directed. This is one of the most condescending and irritating gestures available and should be used sparingly if at all.
- In shaking hands, the position of the hands can communicate dominance or submission. An upturned palm can signal a submissive attitude; a downturned palm, dominance. If you want to give someone else control, extend your hand with the palm facing up. If, however, you want to take control, extend your hand with the palm facing downward.

    The glove-style handshake provides an opportunity for the greeter to display trustworthiness. He or she extends both hands, shaking with one hand while clasping the outside of the recipient's hand with the other. This handshake may seem to create a warm feeling; however, when used on a first meeting, the individual will be perceived as nontrusting. Use this style with long-time friends and associates.
- Rubbing hands together quickly usually communicates excitement. When a salesperson rubs his palms together, he communicates that he has products or services that will benefit the buyer. By the same token, when a buyer rubs her hands together, she probably believes she will benefit from the product or service and will likely buy it.
- Fiddling with loose change in your pocket, whether you are listening or talking, indicates a concern for money. In a selling situation, the buyer is likely communicating a concern for how much the product or service costs.
- Someone who is in constant motion or has trouble sitting still may be thinking of something or someone else, or he may be bored. Nervous energy can also communicate fear in an uncomfortable situation such as an interview.

- Clenched hands generally indicate masked hostility or negative attitudes. The degree of hostility is usually indicated by the height of the hands. The greatest hostility is signaled by hands clenched in front of the face.
- Hands placed in the steeple position can have two meanings, depending on how the hands are positioned. The raised steeple is typically used by a speaker, usually a supervisor, and has a domineering effect on whomever is listening. The lower steepled position, on the other hand, shows that someone is listening.

     When the steeple position is used by a buyer in a selling situation, the salesperson must take into account the gestures preceding this motion before interpreting its meaning. When positive gestures have preceded the steeple position, the salesperson can interpret it as a "yes" and may want to begin to close the sale. If negative gestures have preceded it, the salesperson would be foolish to try and close. The buyer is signaling that he is not interested in the product or service.
- Clasping your hands behind your back signals authority and superiority. This position is common among police officers and other authority figures.
- Gesturing with your thumb extended also sends the message of superiority and authority.
- Covering your mouth with your hand communicates that you are lying or lack self-confidence. When a listener covers her mouth while you are talking, she probably thinks you're lying.
- Nose touching often communicates the same message as covering your mouth. Touching or rubbing your nose or slightly below it communicates deceit.
- Rubbing your eyes often means you are trying to avoid looking at someone who is seen as being untruthful.
- Scratching your neck commonly signals uncertainty or lack of agreement.
- Pulling at the back or side of your collar often communicates deceit and the feeling that someone is suspicious of you.
- Putting your fingers in your mouth says you are nervous and need reassurance.

- As a listener, you communicate boredom when you support your head with your hand as if to keep from falling asleep.
- Resting your closed hand on your cheek with the index finger pointing upward usually means you are evaluating what is being said and signaling interest.
- When the index finger is pointing upward and the thumb is supporting the chin, a negative or critical attitude toward the speaker is communicated.
- Chin stroking usually sends a message to the speaker that you are making a decision. A good salesperson should never interrupt a buyer when he is stroking his chin. When chin stroking is followed by a posture of crossed arms and legs, the salesperson has just gotten her answer, and that answer is no. Chin stroking followed by a readiness gesture, however, means the salesperson can ask how the buyer would like to pay for the product or service.
- Rubbing the back of your neck generally sends the same message as pulling your collar and covering your mouth: you're lying. This gesture is also a common signal that the person you are speaking to is a "pain in the neck."
- Scratching the back of your head says you don't understand what is being said.
- Hands and fingers intertwined, especially when you are seated, often communicates that you are deep in thought.
- Slapping your forehead usually communicates that you are not intimidated by someone's pointing out your forgetfulness.
- Straddling a chair or putting something between you and another person, such as a fence, doorway, or car door, essentially means you are protecting yourself. This position is often taken by domineering types. If you want to overcome this situation, try sitting or standing behind the person who is dominating. He will have to change his position to a more vulnerable one.
- Picking at imaginary lint signals boredom or disagreement.
- Tilting your head usually means you are interested in what is being said.
- A neutral position is communicated when your head is up and you nod throughout the conversation in agreement.

- Tilting your head down signals disagreement, a negative attitude, or anger.
- Holding both hands behind your head communicates confidence, control, and/or superiority. When someone reprimands you in this manner, you might want to respond by mirroring the position.
- Readiness and aggressiveness are communicated by placing your hands on your hips. When your feet are placed evenly on the ground, the degree of readiness is greater.
- Readiness can also be communicated in a seated position by leaning forward with your hands on your legs and one foot in front of the other as if to take a step. Supporting your weight on the armrests of your chair commonly signals that you are about to leave.
- Males display aggression in a number of ways. Like women, men size each other up, usually when they are angled away from each other in a relaxed posture. They may place their hands on their hips or their thumbs in their belt. Men in this position are evaluating each other; however, overt conflict is unlikely.
- When, however, two men face each other directly with their feet about shoulder length apart, weight evenly distributed and their hands on their hips or on their belt, a confrontation may be inevitable.

Gestures should be practiced so that they become natural to you. If you find yourself boring your associates or colleagues, you may want to incorporate some gestures to emphasize a point or illustrate a fact. Remember, however, that gestures should draw attention to the idea and not to the gesture. And don't overuse a gesture. Like anything else used in excess, a gesture that is overused loses impact. Finally, make sure the gesture you're using is appropriate to what you're saying. If you give a sweeping hand motion while talking about parts of an idea, you'll confuse your listener(s).

Vary your gestures. If you have glasses, incorporate them comfortably in your conversation or presentation to bring attention to certain points. In going from one idea to the next, try moving your whole body. You might even consider taking a side step when making a transition from one topic to another.

Gestures you use should be a part of you. Practice daily in front of the mirror. Study other people's gestures. Are their gestures reinforcing or illustrating their verbal communication?

When giving a presentation, practice makes perfect, and this goes for gestures, too. Your gestures can help give your audience the desired impression. Consider what action or reaction you want from your audience as you are deciding what gestures to incorporate. Perhaps you want to motivate the audience to follow you and join an organization. In this case you may want to introduce the fist gesture to prompt them. Experiment with gesturing. Not all of the gestures mentioned earlier are right for you. You must determine for yourself which ones are appropriate. If you are shy, using the fist may be contrary to your personality, whereas if you're assertive, others will expect this gesture of you. Practice make perfect!

EXERCISE 1

Practice daily in front of the mirror different gestures that align with your personality. Practice these until you become comfortable with them and are sensitive to them when you are communicating.

....
....
....
....
....

EXERCISE 2

Spend about a few minutes each day watching other people's gestures. What are their gestures saying? Write down your observations. With each person, evaluate whether the gesture was appropriate to his or her verbal communication and personality type.

....
....
....
....
....

FOUR

Space

Of all the nonverbal forms of communication, I believe space is the most important. Why? The implications of the space around us extend far beyond our personal boundaries to affect us from a social perspective. At one point or another in your life you've probably felt uncomfortable when someone was standing or sitting too close to you. I wonder whether one of the reasons for the high crime rates in our cities has not been a lack of space in which to function comfortably.

Each of us has sacred boundaries, a sort of invisible bubble enclosing us. Any uninvited penetration of this bubble results in anger, violence or movement away to regain the space. In the animal kingdom this space is called "territory" and is guarded jealously.

People are not so different. When two people are dining, they will instantly stake out their territory as one half of the table. If you put something on your companion's half, she will begin to feel uncomfortable. A sense of territory can also come from familiarity. Someone who frequents a restaurant and sits in the same place each time will begin to attribute ownership to that table. Asked where he would like to sit, he may reply, "my usual" or "my table," and if his usual seat is unavailable, he may become quite uneasy.

People claim ownership to other kinds of space as well. You "claim" your desk by putting pictures of your loved ones on it, or other memorabilia. Even at home, family members display ownership of specific pieces of furniture and areas of the house. A father may have "his chair" in which only he sits. Mother may have her study or office.

When you are driving a car, your personal space includes your car and then some, and when someone cuts in front of you, your reaction is the same as if that person had intruded on your personal space without consent. The car, like an office desk, acts as a protective buffer between you and those around you.

Personal space, like other nonverbal communication, is culturally defined. In North America, Australia, and England, the bubble that surrounds people is greater than in France, Italy, and the Arab and Latin American countries. This can lead to problems between people of different cultural backgrounds. The Frenchman, standing close to the American, feels comfortable at that distance and is insulted when the American moves away. However, the American is insulted because the Frenchman has penetrated his intimate space without consent.

Space is also influenced by gender. Two women conversing feel comfortable standing close to one another, while two men will stand further apart. If a man stands too close to another man, the reaction may be similar to that of animals, or the other man will move away to regain his territorial space.

However, when two members of the opposite sex are involved in conversation, the distance between them communicates the nature of their relationship. When you are interested in someone, you will stand very close to that person. If the person is also interested, he will allow you to stand or sit near him. Couples in conversation will stand very close to one another, and each will be perfectly comfortable with the proximity of his or her partner. But when one of the people involved is not interested in the other's advances into "her" space, she will move away—or even make a comment like, "Get away from me!"

According to some researchers, people who grow up in rural areas require more personal space than urban dwellers. People who grow up in country towns require less space than those from rural areas but more space than city folks. By observing how others greet one another, you can tell something about where they grew up. Native city dwellers will stand about one-and-a-half feet away from each other to extend a handshake. Those from country towns will stand at a greater distance apart and lean toward each other with their hand extended. Those from rural or remote areas are comfortable waving to someone they know. Given this information, a salesperson who serves clients from different areas should be sensitive to personal space requirements and not intrude on clients' territory or penetrate their boundaries.

Our space is very important to us, and the distance between people communicates the level of their relationship. Dr. Edward Hall has identified four zones. These vary by culture, but here we will define them according to American standards. The first is referred to as the *intimate zone*. It represents an area approximately zero to eighteen inches from our bodies. This space is heavily guarded and protected, and permission to enter is highly selective. Penetration into this space by anyone other than our partner, family, close friends, or relatives is a violation and may signal hostility or even violence. Rape is an extreme example of intrusion into this intimate zone, as is any physical attack. Because it infringes on one's intimate zone, the effects of such trespassing are felt long after the fact.

The next zone is referred to as the *personal zone*. This zone ranges from one-and-a-half to four feet from the body. Within this zone are two subzones, the close personal and the far personal. The close personal zone extends from one-and-a-half to four feet, the far personal from two-and-a-half to four feet. The close personal zone is reserved for particularly close friends and/or spouse. It is also a comfortable distance during cocktail parties and other friendly gatherings.

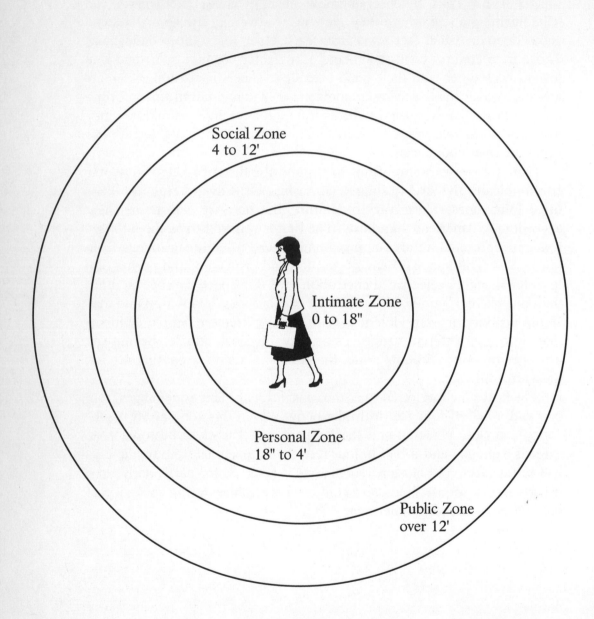

Social Zone
4 to 12'

Intimate Zone
0 to 18"

Personal Zone
18" to 4'

Public Zone
over 12'

The far personal zone puts more distance between people, though they are still close enough for personal conversation. The messages communicated by this distance can be several. At a formal function where people are unfamiliar with one another, allowing someone to enter your far personal zone is usually a way of saying you have singled that person out for better acquaintance. In such a case, if the person in question moves too quickly into your close personal or intimate zone, he or she will be considered pushy. On the other hand, at friendly gatherings where everyone knows everyone else, keeping someone in the far personal zone commonly signals that that person is not to be trusted.

The next zone is called the *social zone.* The distance between people in this zone is from four to twelve feet apart, the distance we stand from repairmen, strangers, the new employee at work, and so on. Dr. Hall divides this zone into two subzones as well: the close zone and the far zone. The close zone—from four to seven feet—is the distance we use in business meetings, with clients, or with repairmen. Employers will often distance themselves this length from subordinates to communicate dominance.

The far zone of social distance, from seven to twelve feet, is common in formal social and business functions. For example, when the president of the United States arrives at a foreign country for a state visit, the atmosphere is formal, so the distance between participants represents the far zone of social distance. A married couple may put this much distance between each other in order to relax after a hard day at work.

Offices and the furniture in them can function to establish this distance between people. For example, a receptionist may have a windowed area for receiving visitors, but the visitors do their waiting in a room distant enough that the receptionist can conduct her work. The boss's desk may be large enough to set this distance between herself and subordinates, communicating that she is the boss and they are the employees.

The last zone Dr. Hall defines is the *public zone.* The public zone is anything over twelve feet. It is firmly established when speakers address a group. Again, Hall describes two subzones: the close zone, which ranges from twelve to twenty feet, and the far zone, which is over twenty feet. The close zone is common during informal gatherings or when people are speaking to groups they know. The close public zone is used when a teacher lectures to students and when the boss is having a meeting with employees.

The far zone is common when someone is speaking to an unfamiliar group, such as a politician giving a campaign speech to a group of voters.

Given all this, how do people respond in crowded situations? Being in a crowd, whether at a concert or in an elevator, represents an intrusion on our personal, sometimes intimate space. In American society there are unspoken laws governing our behavior in crowds, laws that reflect the problem of space. First, we must avoid eye contact. Thus, when getting on a crowded elevator, we find ourselves looking or staring at the floor numbers in order to avoid eye contact. Second, we should not speak to one another. Thus, in the same crowded elevator you might hear a brief "Excuse me," followed by silence. Third, you must not show emotion, maintaining, essentially, a "poker face." Fourth, you must inhibit your body movements. Think of a crowded dance floor. Most people will limit their movement, depending on how crowded it is. When a couple fails to follow the rules and moves about freely, others around them become uncomfortable and try to move away from them. Finally, if someone in a crowded situation has a book or newspaper, he must be totally engrossed in it. This behavior permits avoiding everyone around him.

Because our personal territory is so important to us, any unwelcome penetration of it, even a seemingly friendly touch, may result in hostility or violence. Someone who has a habit of touching others even on a first meeting invites a negative impression. In America, touching is limited as compared to other countries. In business, it is often reserved to the handshake.

However, touching communicates different messages depending on *how* we touch. Richard Heslin divided touch into five categories: functional/professional, social/polite, friendship/warmth, love/intimacy, and sexual arousal. Functional or professional touch refers to the contact made when a doctor examines a patient. Essentially, this category of touch is part of the job function. Social or polite touch is to reaffirm one's identity as a part of the group and is commonly demonstrated by the handshake. The third category of touch is similar to the second category but on a one-to-one level. The love or intimacy category of touch refers to touch that expresses emotional attachment to another human being, such as with a mother to her daughter and a grandparent to grandchild. The fifth category of touch, sexual arousal, refers to touch that affirms emotional attachment through sexual intimacy, as between a husband and wife.

Touching can be interpreted in a positive or negative manner at the workplace. The most common form of touching is the handshake, but other forms can send a message of support and encouragement to an employee. These include touching the shoulder or arm. Hugging employees is inappropriate, however, because hugging is reserved for special friends. By the same token, touching someone at the waist may be interpreted as an unwanted sexual advance. Touching may also be interpreted as condescending. A light pat on the head or shoulder may seem to be patronizing the recipient rather than showing warmth. It's better to be safe than sorry—and to refrain from *all* forms of touching outside of the handshake.

According to Mary Munter, status can be derived from the use of space in seating arrangements. The head of the table is often associated with the group leader, the head of the household, the host, or the most dominant member of the group. Frequent talkers like to have people close to them. When two people are seated at opposite ends of a table, they may well be in competition; think of chess players. When one person sits at the head of the table and the other sits next to her, this seating arrangement is associated with conversational cooperation. But when two people are seated apart from one another, perhaps one at the end of the table and the other at the middle, conversation is inhibited. This seating arrangement generally means non-communication.

EXERCISE

Each day, take a few minutes to observe how others define their space around them. The point of this exercise is to become sensitive to the signals others are sending through the space around them. Observe business associates and the space between them. Observe the role that furniture and the size of offices play in establishing distance between individuals.

....

....

....

FIVE

Voice

The sound of the voice has implications that reach far beyond the words actually communicated. It is not necessarily the words we use but how we say those words that spur action, feelings, or mood. This so-called tone of voice is referred to as *paralanguage*.

Take the simple question, "How old are you?" If we put the emphasis on different words in this sentence, we'll come up with different meanings. Disc jockeys are very sensitive to how their voices come across on the radio. A voice may conjure up visual images of a tall, dark, and handsome man, though in reality it belongs to a short, overweight, nearsighted male.

The sound of your voice has tremendous impact. Your voice communicates your emotional state to others. It can reveal what kind of person you are, warm and friendly or cold and distant. It can also bore or excite your audience. People who speak in a monotone tend to bore their listeners quickly. Motivational speakers are trained to vary their tone to excite their listeners.

In businesses where many transactions take place over the telephone, such as sales, tone of voice can make or break you. When someone calls a business for information or to purchase a product, the sound of the voice on the other end of the line will give the caller a mental image of the nature of the organization, the degree of professionalism of its employees, and the level of service they extend to their customers. For this reason, employers should give as much consideration to the receptionist they hire as they do to employees who will be interacting with customers face-to-face. A pleasant-sounding voice will conjure up positive images; a cold, distant voice, negative ones.

Pets are acutely aware of the sound or tone of your voice. Commands given to a pet are based on tone more than the actual words, and some pets understand our moods through the sound of our voice. This is also true of infants. They may not understand the words that we use, but they can sense our mood by our tone of voice.

Research continually demonstrates that in first impressions, the words we use account for only about 7 percent of the impression we make. Body language, including voice, account for 38 percent, with the remaining 55 percent attributable to visual cues such as dress and physique.

When you are talking on the telephone for the first time with a prospective client, that person does not have the opportunity to look you over, with the result that the sound of your voice becomes increasingly important. Remember this, and use your voice to project what you want it to.

There are several elements of speech that, when used effectively, can enhance the message you want to get across. Pitch, or inflection, is probably the most important. Pitch refers to the tone of the voice. It should be neither too high nor too low, and it should be varied to prevent a monotone effect.

The second element of speech is voice quality. Does your voice have a nasal, harsh, or shallow sound? You can enhance your voice quality with the help of a speech instructor. This is particularly important for women who have a high-sounding voice, since such a voice can detract from an overall impression of credibility and confidence to do the job.

The third element of voice is intensity. Intensity is the loudness of your voice or your ability to project your voice. A really loud person drives others away. But if someone is so soft-spoken that he is actually difficult to hear, his listeners may become frustrated and tune him out. Moreover, a soft-spoken person may not be able to command authority or credibility with subordinates and clients.

The next element of voice is rate. Rate refers to how quickly you speak. Speak too quickly and no one will be able to understand you; too slowly and you may put your audience to sleep. I knew a gentleman who spoke so quickly that he had to repeat each sentence about three times before I comprehended what was said. Not being able to understand someone can be frustrating for the listener. He or she may block you out completely as a result.

The final element of voice is pause. Pausing can be a useful tool to give emphasis to certain points. Constant pausing, however, frustrates the listener, who may get the impression that you aren't sure of what you want to say.

Some voice problems are so distracting that they seriously interfere with communication. A common problem is the overuse of filler words such as "uh" and "you know." One way to cure this habit is to tape yourself. People are often unaware of how frequently they use filler words. When they play back the tape, the surprise they experience is sufficient grounds for self-improvement.

Another common vocal problem is the voice drop. The speaker lets the last few words of a sentence trail off until listeners cannot hear. I'm sure you have encountered this frustrating syndrome in others. Again, taping yourself speaking will bring this problem to the forefront if you suffer from it unknowingly. Breathing techniques are one way to correct a habitual voice drop. Proper breathing will allow all the words you say to be heard. This technique can be learned from a speech or voice instructor.

Another common voice problem is faulty pronunciation. If you don't know the proper pronunciation of a word, don't use it until you learn. In sales, deals can be broken simply on the mispronunciation of the client's name. In social settings, mispronunciation of words or names can be insulting to the listener and embarrassing to you. Practice an unfamiliar word or sound until it becomes part of your vocabulary.

Another common voice problem is poor enunciation. This means the speaker does not articulate well, making it difficult to understand the message. Again, tape yourself and listen to your enunciation. Does "want to" sound like "wanna?" Does "supposed to" sound like "posa?" Can you be understood? If your enunciation is questionable, practice by reading out loud. Effective enunciation stems from enunciating the consonants properly, not just the vowels.

Here are some other tips about voice.

- Your vocabulary says a lot about what kind of person you are. Avoid foul language and slang in your vocabulary even if you hear others using it. The English language has plenty of words to chose from. You may have a beautiful-sounding voice, but foul language and slang will invariably detract from it.

- Have a good grasp of grammar. A pleasant-sounding voice is undercut by the wrong use of a verb tense, pronoun, or other incorrect uses of the English language. If you feel unsure, sign up for an English class to brush up on your language skills. A thorough understanding of the English language will contribute to your success.

Realize that in today's business world, appointments and sales are made by phone. If the person on the other end of the line doesn't like the sound of your voice, that person won't get the message. Let the caller hear energy and enthusiasm and he or she will be motivated to see you or buy your product.

EXERCISE

Tape yourself speaking and play the tape back, or ask your friends or co-workers to critique your voice. Record what you've discovered in a notebook. Then, next to each weakness, state how you intend to correct it. Practice each day for about 15 minutes—or sign up for an English course or voice lessons at a local high school or college. Tape yourself again after the first month, three months, and six months of practice.

....
....
....
....

SIX

Clothing Language

ow you move in your clothing, and how you wear it are a crucial part of the image you project. It is not necessarily what you wear all the time but how you attend to your clothing in the presence of others that communicates respect, authority, position, and status.

We have seen how individual parts of our body communicate messages to others. How we use clothing affects the way others respond to us. It communicates our respect and cooperation and the way we approach others. The tips that follow are applicable to men and women in any profession, but are particularly important to those in marketing and sales.

- When approaching your boss or superior, have your jacket on and buttoned.
- When working in your office, you can take off your jacket and roll up your sleeves; however, if your boss, superior, client, or other important person walks into your office, put it back on.
- Wearing running shoes to a party after work or in the office insults your host and your boss.
- Don't brag about the designer label you're wearing; most people will never have heard of it. (Wait for someone who is genuinely interested to ask you.)

- If you live in a country town and you're from the city, don't dress up in a cowboy hat, boots, huge belt buckle, and jeans. It's probably not you, and others will pick up on that right away.

- If you are a woman, a business cocktail or dinner party calls for conservative dress, not a dress with deep cleavage or a slit up to the thigh. Men, this is not the opportunity to wear your most fashion-conscious or sexy attire either.

- If you are in sales, it's important that customers and potential clients perceive you as approachable. Therefore, when calling on people whose dress is likely to be less formal than what you would ordinarily wear, dress down a little. Let's say you are visiting men on a construction site. Forget the pinstriped suit. You will make a better impression if you wear a long-sleeved shirt, slacks, and appropriate shoes.

- If you are quite the fashion plate, tone down this talent when dealing with a new client. Dress modestly at first; then, once you have established the relationship, gradually return to your regular style. The point is to avoid intimidating a prospective or newly acquired client. You don't have to dress plainly—just toned down a bit.

- If you are the boss, company executive, or the president of the corporation, go out to the work site or to pay a visit to a client dressed to the hilt; it is expected of you. Again, it is a question of image.

EXERCISE

Review the points regarding clothing language. Which ones have you violated? If none, great. If you do have some to work on, pick one rule each week and try to incorporate it into your business attire and behavior.

....
....
....
....
....
....
....

An Overview of Body Language

NONVERBAL BEHAVIOR	INTERPRETATION
Brisk, erect walk	Confidence
Standing with hands on hips	Readiness, aggression
Sitting with legs crossed, foot kicking slightly	Boredom
Arms crossed on chest	Defensiveness
Walking with hands in pockets, shoulders hunched	Dejection
Hand to cheek	Evaluation, thinking
Touching, slightly rubbing nose	Rejection, doubt, lying
Rubbing the eye	Doubt, disbelief
Hands clasped behind back	Anger, frustration, apprehension
Locked ankles	Apprehension
Head resting in hand, eyes downcast	Boredom
Rubbing hands	Anticipation
Sitting with hands clasped behind head, legs crossed	Confidence, superiority
Open palm	Sincerity, openness, innocence
Pinching bridge of nose, eyes closed	Negative evaluation
Tapping or drumming fingers	Impatience
Steepling fingers	Authoritative
Patting/fondling hair	Lack of self-confidence; insecurity
Tilted head	Interest
Stroking chin	Trying to make a decision
Looking down, face turned away	Disbelief
Biting nails	Insecurity, nervousness
Pulling or tugging at ear	Indecision

EXERCISE

PART TWO: DRESS

The Clothes We Wear

PEOPLE OF MANY NATIONS AND CULTURES adorn their bodies to communicate association with certain tribes, religions, or clubs. Adornment comes in many forms and includes clothing, body painting and makeup, jewelry, and accessories.

In social or business settings, clothing acts as a communicator of ourselves, our company, and our position, as well as having the functions already listed. It is not hard to see why appearance constitutes 55 percent of the first impression we make on others.

In job interviews about 75 percent of the decision to hire is based on the applicant's appearance. If you are inappropriately dressed for an interview, you are unlikely to be hired. Inconsistencies in an otherwise professional appearance, such as unpolished shoes or wrinkled pants, will send the interviewer an inconsistent message decreasing your likelihood of being hired. For those of you who *have* recently been hired, it might interest you to know that there is likely to be an eight to twenty percent variation in entry-level salary received based on personal appearance. If you are employed and want to move up the corporate ladder, you will need to communicate this fact not only verbally but also through your appearance.

Given all this, the impression you make is crucial, especially during first meetings. Believe it or not, people size up others within the first three or four seconds of an encounter. Within thirty seconds at least eleven assumptions are made about the other person, including social status, economic status, educational attainment, occupation, marital status, educational status, ancestry, trustworthiness, credibility, and likelihood to succeed. This process is an unconscious one. Yet the reason we do it is simple. In the course of one day we encounter hundreds of things, places, and people, and in order to process all this information quickly we must categorize our encounters based on minimal knowledge. With people it is their appearance that tells us whether or not we want to continue the association.

Researchers have found that people are attracted to others based on their appearance. When someone is dressed similarly to ourselves, we infer that they have similar beliefs, values, attitudes, and even political affiliation, and so are attracted to them.

If all of this seems somewhat—well—fatalistic, here is a more positive note: *Impression management*. This term refers to the process of dressing in a way that controls the impressions you make on others. This process reflects our self-perceptions and the motivations for our behavior. In a word, we have the opportunity to dress so that the impressions others form of us are the impressions we *want* them to form.

I want to say here that this book is not another dress-for-success instruction manual. It does not tell you what you should look like. Instead, it is about attitude. The look of success in the nineties and the next century means communicating your individuality within the guidelines of what is appropriate attire. A lot has changed since the seventies and eighties when women wore navy-blue suits and men wore tailored suits, white shirts, and conservative ties. For women today there are plenty of role models in upper management who dress well while still managing to express their individuality. Women have also had an impact on what is considered appropriate attire for men. In the glamour professions, for example, men can choose the kinds of unstructured suit styles introduced by the television show *Miami Vice*. For men, as well as women, there is a lot of room for self expression.

Why is expressing your individuality so important? Because it communicates creativity and leadership potential. It shows that you know who you are and are confident in yourself and your abilities. Women who dress like men, in gray pinstripe suits, little bow ties, and hemlines way below the knee, are seen as junior executives with no sense of style. Is that what you want to say about yourself?

You need not be a fashion expert to develop your own individual style. Like anything else, however, it takes practice. Work on your clothing style daily. Take time during the weekends to experiment and develop new combinations and looks. By using the guidelines presented in this book, and by doing the exercises, you can develop that look that says you and *only* you!

Ask yourself this: "What messages do I communicate about myself to peers, colleagues, associates, and my boss in the clothing I wear? Do I communicate professionalism and seriousness about the work I do, and do I command respect and confidence in my abilities and position?" These issues can only be addressed by you and will take time to think through.

In the chapters that follow we will address the issues of clothing, jewelry, accessories, and makeup from both a business and a social perspective, since business is often more than nine to five. We will address these concerns differently for men and women, since they have different needs. Read on, and have fun!

SEVEN

Elements for Success

When it comes to executive image, either in or out of the office, the first thing most people think of is money. People who can't afford to are afraid they are going to have to buy a whole new wardrobe. It's just not so. Most Americans—in fact, most people around the world—are just trying to make ends meet, living from paycheck to paycheck. And with inflation, it's a good bet that prices will continue to climb. Plain and simple, clothing is expensive!

My own case is typical. I still calculate every purchase of clothing in relation to what I already own. I can't just go out and buy anything I want (say, like a new outfit that doesn't match anything in my closet). Most people can't go out and buy anything they want when the demands of raising children, saving for college, buying a house, car, or furniture, and paying for medical costs are pulling for every dollar.

That is why I suggest you build your executive wardrobe on the key pieces you already own. Building a wardrobe gives you the opportunity to make wise, well-thought-out clothing investments, just as if you were investing in real estate or mutual funds. But first things first. Before we start to build anything, we must *get organized*! Here are the successful elements of any wardrobe, beginning with organization.

Organize Your Closet

Pull out anything that hasn't been worn in at least a year or that no longer fits. You must have a workable wardrobe. Take the unusable items and give a donation to your favorite charity, or take them to a consignment store. If you have gained a few pounds and continue to hold on to some things because you are planning to loose the weight, give them away. By the time you do lose it, you will want a new wardrobe.

Group your clothing according to category and function. For example, put work clothes in one group and party clothes in another. Put jackets together, skirts together, pants together, shirts and blouses together, sweaters together, sport coats and blazers together, and so on. Group shirts and blouses by sleeve length as well—short and long.

Now arrange these clothing groups by color from light to dark. Include patterns, stripes, and prints as well as your solids.

Select a Color Scheme

From organizing your closet, you'll be able to determine the colors you are most attracted to. This will help you in creating a look all your own. Build your wardrobe around your most common or favorite neutral.

The neutrals are:

— Black
— White (for social only)
— Off-white (or winter white)
— Gray
— Navy
— Camel, beige, khaki, or taupe
— Olive

Accent the neutrals with splashes of color and prints in your shirts, ties, blouses, jackets, pants, skirts, and accessories. For example, a wardrobe based on black can incorporate a glen plaid (banker's plaid) print jacket in black and white. Introduce bright colors like fuchsia and turquoise in blouses, jackets, and accessories.

Invest in Classics

The essence of the executive image is classic styling, simplicity that will last for years to come. Classics are always available and always in fashion. They include tailored suits, navy blazers, ivy-league ties, and button-down oxford shirts, for men, and tailored suits, shirtwaist dresses, tailored notched-collar blouses, a-line skirts, pleated skirts, and cardigan sweaters, for women. There are many many more classic styles currently on the market; skim the fashion magazines and shop windows to become aware of the classics reintroduced each season.

There are also classics in patterns, including tartan plaids, glen plaids, scotch plaids, herringbone, tweed, houndstooth, liberty prints, chalk stripes, and pin stripes. These have been around for years and will continue to be popular for years to come.

Buy the Best

No one is saying you should contribute to our national deficit, or to yours; you should, however, consider your priorities when it comes to your clothing budget. If you can't buy the best party outfit *and* the best clothing for your job, there will have to be a trade off. So consider your priorities. When your priority is your job, allocate most of your clothing budget to those purchases. When that St. Patrick's Day party comes along and you need a green shirt, don't spend a lot of money on it; that's not a priority purchase.

We will talk further about quality in a later chapter, but for now remember this:

**MOST EXPENSIVE DOES NOT MEAN BETTER QUALITY!
NEITHER DOES A DESIGNER LABEL!**

Keep in mind that you can get high-quality garments at most price points and at most department stores and mass merchandisers.

Plan Your Wardrobe Around Separates

This is easier for women, but it's an option that's growing for men too. Separates offer the most mileage for any wardrobe. For women, dresses and jacket dresses provide a great alternative for the office, but you'll get the greatest variety from separates. For example, by breaking apart a black suit you can wear the black skirt with a red double-breasted jacket or a black, white, and red houndstooth Chanel jacket. Adding jackets and skirts to your wardrobe is less expensive than buying suits regularly.

Men in middle to upper-level management still consider the business suit the appropriate office attire; however, sport coats and blazers with coordinating trousers are also acceptable. A navy blazer with gray trousers is a common sight in the office, as is a camel colored sport coat and brown trousers. Or you might consider a linen or raw silk muted plaid sport jacket with coordinating trousers for summer.

Some may argue that the piecemeal approach to creating a wardrobe will result in a piecemeal look, but this isn't true. By organizing your closet and building around the neutrals you can determine the key piece that will pull your wardrobe together, multiplying your choices so that you don't need to buy a whole new wardrobe. Suits are fine for work and for attending social functions, but people today want choices. We all know what it's like to look in the closet and scream, "I haven't got a thing to wear!" When this happens to you, take it piece by piece.

Coordinate Patterns

If you looked through the pages of *House and Garden* back in the sixties and seventies, the decorator's theme usually came across in a patterned couch, solid-colored walls, a solid-colored carpet and drapes, and maybe mildly textured accessory chairs. Look through current issues and what do you see? Florals, stripes, and prints all in the same room—and it looks fantastic!

Our eyes have become accustomed to seeing this mixture not only in our homes but in our clothing as well. Men have been mixing patterns for years when they coordinated patterned ties with patterned suits or shirts. So try coordinating patterns in your wardrobe. Try putting together a patterned scarf and a patterned jacket. The following rules of thumb will make your effort a success:

■ One pattern should dominate. You don't want two or three patterns fighting for first place. Look at the patterns and determine which one jumps out at you first.

■ The patterns should have some colors in common. Commonality in color suggests that the patterns were meant to be together. If it's just one color—fine; more than one—great!

Choose Year-Round Fabrics

Your executive style should emphasize all-season fabrics and colors for year-round wear, particularly if you travel extensively. Some fabrics identify a season, such as wool flannel for fall and winter months and seersucker for spring and summer. However, consider wool gabardine for your suits, pants, jackets, and skirts. Wool gabardine, in a tropical-weight wool, can be worn at any time of year; yes, even in the summer!

In warm climates, tropical-weight wools are common. In the north and in the midwest, you'll find heavy-weight wools for winter and lighter-weight ones for summer. Tropical-weight or medium-weight wools are superb for any climate any time of year.

When choosing fabrics, choose natural fibers or natural fibers blended with a synthetic. For example, cotton shirts blended with polyester should be about 65 percent cotton and 35 percent polyester. With wool you could go as high as 50 percent wool, 50 percent polyester, and still maintain a natural look while avoiding the cost of 100 percent wool. Some other fabrics to consider include silk, cotton, and rayon. Here is some basic information about these fibers.

■ Silk: Silk is one of the most luxurious fibers today. It has good elastic recovery, so it won't lose its shape over time. In addition, it is highly absorbent, which makes this fiber cool for summer wear.

■ Cotton: Cotton is an easy-care fiber appropriate for winter and summer, depending on the weight of the fabric. Cotton is highly absorbent and therefore comfortable for summer wear, but it is also warm for winter, as countless cotton sweaters and sweatshirts attest.

- Rayon: A popular fabric today, rayon is half-natural and half-synthetic. Blended with natural fibers it can offer easy-care properties not found with 100 percent rayon products.

Get the facts on fibers and fabrics before buying. Become a responsible consumer and know how to care for the fabrics you purchase. If you prefer to avoid dry-cleaning, focus on natural fibers blended with synthetics; or, if you're considering buying silk or rayon, choose washable varieties.

Accessorize

Accessories are the key to creating and expressing your individuality. Moreover, when you open your closet and find you "haven't got a thing to wear," they can help you create a whole new look relatively cheaply.

After all, investing in accessories is a lot less expensive than buying a suit or jacket. Department stores realize that consumers are often in need of a pick-me-up in their wardrobes but don't necessarily have a great deal of money to spend. This is particularly true during a recession. You might observe that the square footage allocated to accessories grows in tough times, accommodating consumers' desires for something new at modest prices.

Accessories are just as important to completing the total look for men as they are for women. Men's accessories include ties, ascots, handkerchiefs, tie pins, wrist watches, shoes, socks, belts, shirts, and glasses. Changing a shirt or tie can be the ticket to a new look with the same suit. Instead of a button-down oxford shirt with a sport coat, try a turtleneck or mock turtleneck—or a polo shirt, for that matter. The well-dressed man makes use of available accessories to add that extra polish to his clothing ensemble.

For women, accessories include scarves, shoes, hosiery, glasses, hats, handbags, gloves, jewelry, and belts. Changes in accessories can take an outfit from day to evening with minimal effort. For example, if you are wearing a black chemise with a red jacket, accessorize for day with gold earrings, a black patent-leather belt, black patent-leather pumps, an interesting broach on the lapel of the jacket, and a scarf. For evening, remove the jacket, step into some high-heeled sandals in black fabric, remove the belt and scarf, and add dramatic gold earrings and necklace or pearl earrings and multiple-strand choker pearl necklace. You're ready for the evening—and you're on time!

When considering accessorizing your clothing ensembles, avoid excessive jewelry. Men, the only jewelry you need is a good watch and your wedding band. Women, don't go overboard with rings on every finger and ankle bracelets. Furthermore, and this goes for everybody, when accessorizing with gold or silver, stick with one or the other. If you're wearing gold earrings or cufflinks, make sure your chain or tie clip is gold too.

Keep your figure proportions in mind when accessorizing. A petite person should wear modestly sized jewelry and belts. People of larger stature and proportions can wear large jewelry and accessories. Accessories used in moderation add glamour to any outfit; too many add confusion.

Take time to experiment. Some day when you have fifteen minutes or half an hour, pull out some outfits and accessorize them. Stuck? Perhaps you have a friend who can help you with this. By all means, make it a social occasion! If you have a hard time remembering what went with what, write it down in a notebook and refer to your notes when you need to.

By setting aside the time to plan and accessorize your outfits, you can save time later. You can also determine what you need in the way of jewelry and other things, and budget for them.

Maintain Your Wardrobe

Part of keeping a great wardrobe together is maintaining it. Some people love to buy new clothes but never take care of what they have. Clothes are not meant to last forever, but without proper maintenance your clothing will fall apart sooner than it should, or end up looking second-rate. Maintaining your wardrobe includes polishing your shoes, washing or dry-cleaning your clothes, shining jewelry, mending garments, ironing or pressing as needed, and cleaning and repairing scarves, belts, handbags, briefcases, handkerchiefs, and so on.

Invest in a shoe cloth and wipe shoes before wearing them. When shoes show wear and tear, such as worn heels or soles, or scuff marks, have them repaired. A person meeting you for the first time looks at shoes as much as the rest of your outfit when collecting cues about who you are and what kind of a person you are. If your outfit is beautiful but your shoes are scuffed and dirty, you'll communicate an inconsistent message about yourself. Fine-quality polished shoes communicate your association with and kinship to fine-quality people.

I asked a bank president how he would feel if a customer came in for a loan or to conduct other major business looking great from head to ankle but with scuffed, unpolished shoes. He said he would be cautious. Why? Because the person had overlooked the details of his appearance.

When caring for your clothing, read the care labels diligently. In fact, read them before you purchase the clothing so that the care of the garments is in line with what you can afford. If you cannot afford high dry-cleaning bills, don't purchase items that must be dry-cleaned. The care label instructions have usually been tested to represent the most effective way of cleaning the garment without damaging it. If you choose to clean your wardrobe your own way, you may be jeopardizing your investment.

Whether you work in a uniform or jeans, your wardrobe must be in tiptop condition. What you wear should be clean, wrinkle free, and in good condition. If your uniform is torn, mend it. If your work jeans are frayed at the hem and pockets, buy a new pair. Whatever you wear should be in the best condition possible so that you can put your best foot forward in any setting.

Pick a Suitable and Manageable Hairstyle

Today's active lifestyle doesn't include fussing with your hair, so select a hairstyle appropriate for your hair type, face, lifestyle, profession, and personality. When choosing your hairstyle, seek the guidance of a professional hairdresser. And pick a hairdresser you can trust! Easier said than done, you say? Yes, but there is a difference between a good haircut and a bad one. In both cases you leave the hairdresser's looking great. Only when it's *your* turn to fix your hair does the difference becomes apparent. A good hairdresser will cut your hair in such a way that when it's your turn to style it, your hair falls right into place. With a bad haircut, you may spend hours searching for the same look you had when you left, and never find it. Alas, I speak from experience!

Take care of your hair. The condition of your hair eloquently communicates your degree of personal hygiene—essentially, how you feel about yourself. Dry, brittle, bleached-out hair or dandruff tells others that you really don't give your appearance much thought. People may be put off by the condition of your hair.

For both men and women, coloring hair is an option, but seek the advice of a professional hairdresser before doing so. And if you want to change the color, do it gradually. Don't go from blonde to brunette overnight. If you do make the change gradually, the only person who will know that the color is different is you; others will just notice how great you look. Remember, hair color should complement skin and eye color. If you have fair skin and blue eyes, dark brown hair may not be suitable.

As we age our body changes—including our hair and skin color. We begin to lose color in our hair and complexion. Women who use cosmetics may notice these changes earlier, as they find themselves using more lipstick, foundation, blush, and eye shadow to try and draw out their natural coloring. If this applies to you, be careful not to overdo it.

If your hair is graying, you may choose to leave it as is or color it. Just be aware that as your hair grays, it affects the color of your complexion. You may find you have to introduce new colors into your wardrobe or makeup. If you do choose to color your hair, don't keep it the same color it was when you were in high school: lighten it two or three shades. Lightening the hair softens facial wrinkles, while preserving it at the color it was in youth looks harsh and calls attention to the wrinkles.

Facial hair can be a problem for women as well as men. Women, if you have facial hair above the lip or around the ears, consider bleaching these areas rather than shaving them. Shaving will make the hairs coarse and dark.

Men, facial hair should be well-trimmed and clean. If you choose to have a mustache, make sure it is trimmed well above the upper lip so that it doesn't catch your food when you are eating. Long hair is an option for men, but, like short hair, should be clean, in good condition, and shaped. If you can't take the time to care for your long locks, cut them. A good haircut is just as important for men as for women, so seek the services of a professional.

If you are balding or have a receding hairline, you may choose to purchase a hairpiece, get a hair transplant, or make use of other methods for combating hair loss. Whatever you do, however, don't sweep the remaining hair over the bare spot to try and cover it. This only calls attention to your hair loss and the fact that you're not comfortable about it. A good haircutter can give you a cut that creates a new look, a cut that looks great on you.

Skin Care Is Essential, Makeup Is Optional

Living in Florida and Arizona taught me the importance of skin care for both men and women. Caring for your skin from early childhood on will minimize the noticeable signs of aging.

Skin cancer is prevalent throughout America and on the rise. As a teenager and a college student you may have spent hours in the sun for the most gorgeous tan on campus. It was fun at the time, but you pay for that tan, starting sometimes as early as your twenties, with little lines. You may still be paying for that fun in the sun in your thirties, forties, fifties, and sixties—with skin cancer. A person can have several bouts of skin cancer; it can occur anywhere on the body that has been exposed to extensive sunning, and it can be fatal. So use sunscreen lavishly, whether you're fair, olive-complexioned, or dark. Your skin must be protected from ultraviolet rays.

Get in the habit of cleansing, toning and moisturizing your skin. Men have the routine in place when they start shaving. After-shave, if used, acts as a toner. Follow it with a moisturizer suited to your skin type.

Whether you are a man or a woman, seek the services of a cosmetician to learn about your skin type and the kinds of products you should use. Oily complexions should avoid heavy moisturizers and oil based cosmetics. Dry complexions should use moisturizing cleansers, toners, and heavy moisturizers to protect and nourish the skin.

Why is skin care so important? As we age, we lose moisture in our skin. Those of us who started out with oily complexions find that our skin is less oily as we mature. Those who began with normal and dry complexions may find, as we mature, that our skin is becoming taut and overly dry. Facial lines are much more apparent when the skin is dry. So it's important to get in the habit of a skin routine that is suitable for your complexion as well as your lifestyle. You may have to modify the products that you use as you mature, but doing so will save your face in the long run.

A word is in order here about personal hygiene. A daily routine of bathing, applying deodorant, shaving, flossing and brushing your teeth, and washing and conditioning your hair is crucial to being your best. Dirty hair is unbecoming. So is bad breath! Have a dental check-up every six months. Remember, a healthy clean appearance is a must to the executive image.

Cosmetics are something else to think about. Try to bear in mind that they are meant to enhance your appearance, not cover it up. When you are young, your features are distinct and your coloring is strong. The colors you use to enhance your features can also be strong and vibrant. As you mature, your features and coloring become softer, and the colors you use to enhance your beauty should also be softer. Strong colors on a mature face look harsh and painted. Moreover, when applying makeup, blend the colors, don't "paint" your face.

No matter the age, an over-painted face distracts from, rather than enhances, one's beauty. Put makeup on in a well-lit room when dressing for day and in subtle lighting for night. Avoid bright-colored or neon eyeshadows in favor of navies, browns, deep purples and plums, rose, taupe, teals, blue-grays, peaches, and beiges. Choose colors that reflect your coloring. If you're a blue-eyed blonde, consider brown mascara rather than black. If you're a brown-eyed brunette, consider black or chocolate-brown mascara.

Seek professional consultation from a cosmetician regarding the right colors for you. In fact, I would recommend getting advice from several beauty experts. Those who represent a cosmetic line may recommend more makeup than is right for you in order to sell more products. They may also create a look representative of the company's image, such as "sophisticated lady" or "natural sport," rather than a look that represents *you*. Experiment and find out what you're comfortable with. The most important thing to remember is that a made-up face should look as natural as possible. The less makeup the better. Let your inner beauty shine through.

Think Quality and Fit

It's important to be aware of quality and fit cues when investing in clothing. Quality doesn't mean designer apparel, either. No matter what name is on the garment, no matter where you buy it, inspect the merchandise before buying.

I once considered buying an Evan Piccone suit from a prestigious store. When I tried it on and looked in the mirror, I noticed that the color varied slightly between the jacket and skirt. Closer examination showed that indeed, there was a distinct difference between the skirt and jacket. Apparently, the items came from two different dye lots. The time I took to inspect the quality of this suit saved me $230 (this was some years ago).

Be sensitive to fit. The apparel industry doesn't have standardized sizing, so one manufacturer's size 6 may be another's size 10. You may discover, when you try on an expensive garment, that you'll fit a considerably smaller size than you normally wear. This is called "psychological sizing." Manufacturers and designers realize that you are more likely to buy something, even something expensive, when you can wear a size 6 instead of your normal size 10. Men's suits are cut more generously than men's sportswear. So think fit, not size.

You may find that a certain manufacturer's brand fits you well. Great. However, if, occasionally, you try a garment on and it doesn't fit, try another in the same size. Since clothes are made by human beings, variations can crop up.

Individualize Your Executive Image

In choosing the right look for you, be sensitive to how your superiors dress. Ask yourself whether there is an unwritten dress code. Look at your profession, your personality, your lifestyle. Are you an extrovert with a hurried lifestyle? Then the look you choose might be excitingly easygoing. Perhaps you're on the quiet side. In that case you might choose milder colors, styles, and looks. The choices are all yours, to make for yourself. Who knows better than you your likes and dislikes, your figure assets and liabilities, your position, your lifestyle?

Today the look that communicates who you are is the essence of the executive image. It's all right to be fashion conscious and aware of fashion trends, but don't be swayed into acquiring fashions that aren't you. Be yourself and enjoy.

EXERCISE 1

Take a weekend and organize your closet. Use the form below to make an accurate assessment. For example, list your pant styles (such as double-pleated wool pants) under the heading "Pants." Note all appropriate colors, as well. Think about what pieces or accessories will work together well.

Clothing Item   Color

Jackets: ....

....

....

Pants: ....

....

....

Skirts: ....

....

....

Blouses and/or shirts: ....

....

....

Sweaters: ....

....

....

Suits: ....

....

....

Dresses: ....

....

....

EXERCISE

Accessories   Color

Belts: ....
....
....

Scarves: ....
....
....

Handkerchiefs: ....
....
....

Ties: ....
....
....

Shoes: ....
....
....

Hosiery/Socks: ....
....
....

Bags and Briefcases: ....
....
....

Jewelry: ....
....
....

Miscellaneous: ....
....
....

EXERCISE

EXERCISE 2

Personality and Lifestyle Analysis

In the space provided below, analyze your personality, lifestyle, profession, and position. Read over what you have written, then, in the space provided, describe the look that's right for you.

Personality: ....
....
....

Lifestyle: ....
....
....

My likes and dislikes in clothing are: ....
....
....

My figure assets and liabilities are: ....
....
....

My profession is: ....
....
....

My position is: ....
....
....

My job responsibilities are: ....
....
....

EXERCISE

My superiors wear: ....
....
....

❑   ❑   ❑

My executive image can best be described as: ....
....
....

EIGHT

Nine to Five

Your clothing says a lot about you at work. If you're in sales, the clothing ensemble you wear can be the bridge—or the barrier—to reaching a prospective client. Clothing also communicates your position and status in a company. Remember, "If they don't like the messenger, they won't get the message."

Men

Different career paths have different wardrobe requirements. In law, banking, accounting, and other traditional fields, classic suits prevail. In retailing, education, real estate, and sales positions, suits or sport coats and coordinating trousers are worn, while jeans and shirts are better suited to construction and like professions. In glamour fields such as public relations, fashion, art, theater, and interior design, contemporarily styled or unstructured suits may best communicate your expertise. However, no matter what your job or position, your clothing must look its best. Don't wear ragged jeans, a dirty shirt, a wrinkled suit, or beat up shoes. If you wear a uniform, make sure it's clean and pressed for work.

Suits. The best suit to buy is a pure wool or wool blend suit in blue, gray, or beige. The darker the suit, the more authority it conveys. Although brown is commonly worn in the midwest, use this color sparingly. Black is a popular color, but it can make people think of funerals. Consider patterned suits. The most prevalent and authoritative include pin stripes, chalk stripes, and muted plaids, also called glen plaids.

When considering the purchase of a suit, men, take your time. The suit is not only is the most expensive type of garment you will ever purchase, it means a great deal to your executive image. So forget the fifteen-minute shopping spree. Plan ahead and get a feel for what you want. Here are some tips to help you.

- Before shopping for a suit, decide what color, pattern, texture, weight, material, and style of suit you'll need. Settle on the price range and know your approximate size. Some department stores carry suits for a variety of body types as well as sizes. For example, JC Penney has suits for athletic, average, and tall builds. An athletic build is made for someone with a large chest and a small waist. The difference in the chest and waist measurement is referred to as drop. In an average build the drop from the chest to waist is about seven inches; in an athletic build it is greater.

- When shopping for a suit, wear the shoes, belt, and shirt that you plan to wear with the suit.

- Once you find a suit you like, examine it carefully for quality cues. Check the stitching around the collar. Is it neat and reinforced? Check for broken or unmatched buttons and weakly constructed buttonholes. Make sure buttons and buttonholes blend well with the suit color, pattern, and fabric.

  - If the suit is plaid or striped, check at the side, back, and shoulder seams to make certain the patterns line up. Button the coat to check that the pattern is properly aligned in front. Check the suit fabric for resiliency by crushing a piece of the fabric in your hand. If the fabric springs back, it's resilient and will look good through a day of sitting and standing.

- The choice of plain or cuffed bottoms is yours. Just remember that pant length for plain bottoms should break in the front and be one-half to three-quarters of an inch longer in the back. Cuffed bottoms should hang horizontal to the floor. Be sure there are no bulges or wrinkles when the cuff is made.

- Although vests are not as popular as they once were, they are still worn. If you choose to purchase a vested suit, check the fit. The arm-holes should not sag; the back should not wrinkle or ride up during activity. The vest should feel comfortable, too.

- Sleeve length on a jacket should be five inches from the tip of the thumb.

- The best all-season fabric for a suit is wool, followed by wool blends. For summer, however, cotton-blended suits are excellent for warm climates. Avoid knit suits and suits constructed in rayon and nylon fabrics, because they won't last.

- When it comes to the style of the suit, men can choose between the square or the soft-shoulder cut and single or double-breasted. Square-shoulder styles are generally ventless, and more fitted than single-vented soft-shoulder styles.

Sport coats, blazers, and coordinating trousers. Consider these alternatives: a navy blazer with khaki or gray trousers; a camel or beige sport coat with charcoal-brown trousers; a black tweed jacket with charcoal-gray trousers. Whether a sport coat, blazer, or suit jacket, the jacket should be long enough to cover the rear.

Shirts. Shirts are a low-cost choice for changing the look of a suit. A different shirt and tie can give the impression of a whole new outfit. When buying shirts, select 100 percent cotton or cotton blends of 35 to 40 percent polyester and 65 to 70 percent cotton. Most dress shirts are white and solid colored. Blue is the most popular color, followed by other pastels—the lighter the better. However, pink and lavender-colored shirts should be worn with caution, especially around people to whom these colors are likely to communicate the wrong impression. Other tips for choosing the right shirt are as follows:

- Generally, the shirt should be lighter than the suit and the tie should be darker than the shirt.

- When buying shirts, choose pinpoint oxford cloth, end-on-end weaves, and broadcloth fabrics.

- Stripes have become a new classic in men's wardrobes. Single or multi-colored stripes on a single-colored background are best. A simple box plaid is also acceptable. Choose from pin- or chalk-width stripes for your business attire.

■ Short-sleeved dress shirts are unacceptable. It is better to roll up your long sleeves than to be caught wearing short sleeves.

■ Monogramming on shirts should be discreet. The color of the monogramming should be the same color as the shirt and should be sewn on the cuff.

■ When buying, avoid shiny shirts, shirts with translucent weaves, shirts with wavy stripes, and shirts with jacquard, floral, paisley, rug, chain, or washed-out patterns.

■ Be sure the shirt fits comfortably around the collar, back, chest, and arms.

■ The shirt should be long enough that the fifth button of a six-button shirt falls at least three inches below the waistband of the pants.

■ Unless they are button-down, check collars for removable stays.

■ Check that the sleeve length is just below the wrist bone. When worn with a suit, blazer, or sport coat, the shirt sleeve should extend about half an inch below the jacket sleeve.

■ Solid-colored shirts have the greatest ability to coordinate with your whole wardrobe. Consider solid-colored shirts with white collars and cuffs as an alternative.

■ Be sure that buttons are plain, simple, and white.

■ Your shirt wardrobe might include a good dozen white, blue, and pin- or chalk-striped shirts in oxford cloth and broadcloth; however, the number and variety are entirely up to you and the image you want to project.

The Tie. Whether or not we are conscious of it, the tie is one of strongest symbols of respectability and responsibility for a man. Ties communicate who you are, reinforcing or detracting from your otherwise positive image. Although the tie you wear can't guarantee your success, it just might open the door to greater opportunities by the signals it sends.

Executives have different opinions about the function of ties, particularly the so-called power tie. One executive, the president of the marketing division of a marketing research company, always wears a red-patterned tie for important meetings. A senior consultant at another marketing firm wears conservatively-patterned ties to blend with his suits when meeting with prospective clients. The role of the tie in the total image varies for different executives, so you must uncover the role it plays in your image.

Given all this, buying a tie is a serious matter. As the one who will wear the tie, take time to shop for it yourself; don't let your secretary, wife, or girlfriend do it for you. Here are some tips that will make this purchase a success.

- The best fabric for ties is silk, followed by polyester that looks like silk, silk/polyester blends, wool, and cotton.
- Determine the length the tie should be. How tall you are and how you tie your tie will help you figure the tie length; the tie should come to your belt buckle with no more or less to spare. Ties come in two lengths: regular and tall. If you are long-waisted or have a large neck, you may need the extra length in a tall man's tie. If you are short-waisted, you may need to have the tie shortened. Have the person doing the alterations shorten the small end of the tie rather than the large end.
- The width of the tie should harmonize with the width of your suit lapels—wide ties with wide lapels.
- Make sure that the lining of the tie is coarse enough to make a good knot. Silk ties are often too slippery to hold a knot unless they are backed by wool or cotton.
- Check for a tab on the back of the large end of the tie. Since tie clips are rarely used these days, the tab is there to slip the small end through so that it doesn't show.
- For traditional professions, choose from polka dot, paisley, or repetition patterns. Polka dots should be smaller than marbles to create a sophisticated image. The repetition or regimental tie should be patterned with neat clean stripes and in dark colors. However, pastel stripes are acceptable for summer.

  Paisleys, great for spicing up dull suits, are considered a classic. Madras plaid ties are ideal for summer wear, particularly with seersucker or pincord suits. Club-patterned ties feature heraldic shields, sailboats, horses, and so on against a solid background, while Ivy League patterns usually consist of small triangles, circles, and/or diamonds repeated against a solid background.

- If you are in retailing, advertising, real estate, or a nontraditional field or company, consider large florals or ties with large symbols or big pictures. However, avoid ties that show faulty dying and construction techniques. Patterns should be clean and crisp. Depending on your position and the nature of the company where you are employed, you may want to venture into black and purple ties, bow ties, and ties in unusual colors, patterns, shapes, or sizes. However, if you are not sure, stick with the classics.

- Consider solid ties, such as solid blues, pastels, and grays, for variety.

Now let us turn our attention to shoes, accessories and grooming. Men's shoes should include a pair of oxfords and a pair of slip-ons, or loafers. Your shoes should match the color of your belt. You may consider cordovan-colored belts and shoes, since this color goes with most wardrobe neutrals. However, black is better for more formal occasions.

Men's accessories play an important role in creating their total image. They include handkerchiefs, socks, and jewelry, along with the previously discussed shoes, ties, and shirts.

- Handkerchiefs: Become comfortable with buying silk-printed and white cotton or linen handkerchiefs to place in the breast pocket of your jacket. Serving a purely decorative function, this accessory can lend pizzazz to an otherwise dull outfit.

- Socks: Choose from a wide selection of muted patterns. Your socks should match or closely match the color of your pants or shoes. They should also stay up. Avoid loud argyle patterns that call attention to your feet.

- Suspenders: A popular accessory. Consider your company's image as well as your profession and position when choosing patterns and colors. Suspenders should attach to the inside buttons of the pants. Don't wear a belt in addition to suspenders and don't buy clip-on styles.

- Grooming: Whether you are in construction or an IBM executive, personal hygiene is essential. This includes clean and well-groomed hair, clean, healthy-looking nails, well-groomed facial hair, and a clean mouth. Your hair should neither be too long nor too short and should be cut in a manner that suits your hair type, face shape, personality, profession, and position. Clean dry to normal hair at least three times a week and oily hair every day. If you have a scalp problem such as dandruff, treat it immediately.

Sideburns are a no-no in most fields, particularly traditional ones. If you have a beard or mustache, make sure it is groomed daily. In particular, the mustache should be cut well above the upper lip to avoid food collecting in it. In some companies facial hair becomes less acceptable as you move up the corporate ladder. You may want to look to your superiors to see whether this is the case at your job.

Brush and floss your teeth daily. Use an oral rinse after brushing and flossing for extra freshness, and have your teeth checked every six months. Remember, bad breath may be a sign of dental problems. A dry mouth also results in mouth odor, so drink plenty of fluids and chew sugarless gum to moisten your mouth and freshen your breath throughout the day. If your teeth need straightening or whitening, you may want to consider investing in your smile.

Consider your daily hygiene to include a bath, a shave, and deodorant. If you use an after-shave or cologne, don't put on too much. Rule of thumb: If you can smell yourself, you have too much on.

Another crucial area for men is their nails. Nails should be clean, with smooth edges and healthy cuticles. If you don't have time to take care of your nails yourself, have a weekly manicure.

The important thing to remember when creating your executive image is that other people infer the quality of your work from how you look. Give yourself a shot at being the tops in whatever you do through the way you dress. Not only will others perceive you to be credible and likely to succeed, you will feel you're worth it as well.

Women

Fashion for the office was initially a no-no for women; the more mannish they looked, the better. Since then, the dress code has changed. Today it reflects the look of a secure woman rather than a woman imitating a man or a helpless little girl. Even now, however, women who are uncertain of their fashion expectations are often seen in man-tailored suits with conservative appeal. This communicates nothing so much as low self-confidence. It is not that the office has become a place to show off fashion's latest; business is not for extremes. But an updated look has taken hold, a look that reflects fashion trends with conservative overtones.

Like menswear, businesswear for women will vary according to their career and the company they represent. Some companies may have relaxed dress codes, while others remain stringent. Naturally, the career path you choose goes a long way in determining what you wear. If you are employed in the fashion industry, public relations, interior design, or art—the creative or glamour fields—your wardrobe is crucial to communicating your expertise. Dressing with flair through mixtures of patterns and textures, accessorizing with interesting pieces, and incorporating tailored looks in bold colors will help build bridges with your customer or client.

In traditional fields, such as high-tech, law, banking, finance, and accounting, a woman's clothing must reflect the conservative nature of these career paths. However, you should not equate "conservative" with dowdy or pin-striped suits. Suits with interesting cuts and design structures, accompanied by classically styled blouses, give an updated look that communicates expertise and credibility in your profession.

In sales, marketing, and education, you bridge the creative and traditional fields. Here you have the opportunity to add some flair to updated tailored looks. Introduce fine-quality knits and two-piece dresses.

If you're at a company where pants are acceptable attire or in a position that has very relaxed dress codes, don't get too relaxed about your looks. Whatever you wear should be clean, pressed, and in tip-top condition. If you wear a uniform, it should fit properly and be clean, pressed, and in good condition. If you are allowed to wear pants and tops, don't wear frayed or faded jeans, tight tops, or dirty shoes. Look your best in whatever you wear to work and in whatever job you have.

Remember that your credibility and quality of work are perceived in the light of how you look. If you want to create the impression that you are serious about the business and that you know what you're talking about, create that impression instantly in the clothing you wear. Then you won't have to take up valuable time convincing your audience that you're truly a professional. Here are some basics that will get you started on the right track.

- The basic pieces to a women's wardrobe are suits and dresses. However, there are several "in between" alternatives to choose from, including jacket dresses and two-piece dresses. Focus on tailored suits without vests. For more relaxed atmospheres, or for days only, consider pantsuits.
- Choose suits in wool, linen, or rayon blends, good quality polyester (doesn't shine and has shape) or natural fibers blended with synthetics.

  Polyester has become a hot fabric due to technological advances. Suits of this fiber can be light weight and easy care for those who don't have a dry-cleaning budget. However, it may get uncomfortable during summer months since the material doesn't breathe.
- The best patterns for suits are solid, houndstooth, tweed, and plaid.
- The best colors range from navy, to charcoal-gray, black, winter white, olive, teal and khaki. If you are in a semi-traditional or creative field, try purple, mustard, cinnamon, blue violet, and other stronger colors. Avoid pastels. Pastels are perceived as weak, extremely feminine, and not really business oriented. Choose stronger colors or neutrals for work and save the pastels for your own time.

  Green is a difficult color. In certain shades, such as forest green and chartreuse, green is appropriate; however, neon greens and plain greens are best worn, again, on your own time.

Suits. Many suits today have a jacket in one color and a skirt in another. This is a great alternative to the traditional suit and should be considered in your wardrobe.

When you buy a suit, several considerations should be made as to quality, style, and fit. Plan ahead. What color, pattern, texture, weight, material, and style will you need? Decide the price range and know your approximate size.

Women, like men, have several suit styles to choose from. Most common is the soft-shoulder style with loose fit and single vent. Growing in popularity, however, is the square-shoulder suit. This style is fitted and ventless. Women also have the choice of a single or double-breasted suit, which could include a short jacket with a longer gathered skirt, an oversized jacket with a slim skirt, or a no-lapels jacket with a pleated, A-line, or slim skirt. Varieties are endless and make carving out your own look that much easier.

- When shopping for a suit, wear the shoes, belt, and blouse you will be wearing with the suit, or at least have an idea of them.
- Once you find a suit you like, examine it very carefully. Check the stitching around the collar. Is it neat and reinforced? Check for broken, unmatched buttons and weakly constructed buttonholes. A suit should be a lifetime investment, so be sure that buttons and buttonholes are not only well constructed but blend well with the suit color, pattern, and fabric.
- If the suit is plaid or striped, check at the side, back, and shoulder seams to be sure the patterns match along these seams. Button the coat to check that the pattern is properly aligned in front.
- Test the suit fabric for resiliency by crushing a piece of the fabric in your hand. If the fabric springs back, it is resilient and will look good through a day of sitting and standing.
- The skirt should come to right about the knee. This is the most attractive length for women. If you like your skirts a bit shorter, fine, but only one or two inches. The length should be at a point where you can function easily without worrying about it. Don't wear anything lower than midcalf. The look then becomes dowdy, not to mention dangerous: at that length it can get caught in doors and chairs. If you want something past the knee, just below is best.
- If you're fitting pants, the pant length for plain bottoms should break in the front and be one-half to three-quarters of an inch longer in the back. Cuffed bottoms should hang horizontal to the floor. Be sure there are no bulges or wrinkles when the cuff is made.

- Make sure your jacket fits comfortably without pulling, bulging, or sagging. Sleeve length on the jacket should be five inches from the tip of the thumb.
- Blouses should be cut simply with no excess frills or lace. In most cases the color of the blouse should contrast with the suit; however, an alternative that is just as pleasing is a blouse of the same color as the jacket and/or skirt. Consider such blouse styles as a jewel neck, round neck, tailored notched collared styles, banded, draped neck, and cowl neck with long or short sleeves. V-neck-styled blouses are acceptable provided they show no cleavage.

  When wearing a sheer blouse, wear a slip or camisole to conceal your foundation. If your bra shows at the front closing of a blouse, pin it discreetly. Choose blouses in silk, polyester (it looks like silk and has the price of silk in some cases), cotton, ramie, and linen.
- A simple skirt and blouse appear unprofessional and incomplete. Consider an interesting belt, a scarf, and jewelry to give this look a professional polish. Many two-piece dresses are simply a skirt and a blouse and need accessorizing to pull the look together.
- Nowadays pants are acceptable at the work place. Choose pantsuits or trousers and blazers for an alternative professional look; however, when on a job interview, consider a skirt suit over a pantsuit.

Shoes. Stick with a conservative pump. Avoid sling backs, strapped sandals, flats, and extremely high-heeled shoes. The look should be one of professional ease. Buy heels that range from one to two-and-a-half inches. Anything higher affects productivity.

From a medical standpoint, the higher the heel, the worse off your feet. High-heeled shoes promote ingrown toenails and other foot problems. And no wonder: Did you know that the weight exerted on the balls of your feet when you are wearing high heels is at least three time your actual weight? Women who have worn high heels most of their lives end up unable to wear heels at all. So stick to lower-heeled pumps constructed to be easy on your feet, such as Naturalizer Soft Shoes, Naturalizer Sport, Rockports, or Easy Spirit, to name a few. These shoes are constructed with cushioned insoles that resemble the feel and look of athletic shoes, soft leather uppers, and flexible soles.

Focus on pump styles that compliment your outfit rather than drawing attention to your feet. I'm sure you would rather others focused on your best asset, your face. Avoid white and bright-colored pumps. Spectator pumps with combinations of white are OK, but an all-white shoe soils easily and draws attention to your feet. If your feet are large or wide, white shoes will also accentuate these traits. Choose shoes that match or coordinate with your wardrobe neutrals.

If your wardrobe is built around black, have at least two pairs of black pumps so that each pair receives a twenty-four-hour rest between wearings. Furthermore, invest in a shoe cloth and wipe shoes off before wearing. If they look scuffed, polish them or wipe them with a mink oil sponge. Send them to the repair shop when they need it. You might also consider investing in shoe trees in metal, cedar, or plastic to help your shoes retain their shape.

Accessories. Accessorize to send the message of individuality and presence. Accessories are the key to pulling a look together and putting your stamp on it. They give a polished look to your executive image. Accessories include jewelry, hosiery, belts, scarves, handbags, and briefcases.

Limit jewelry to gold, silver, or pearls. Adding a little glitter to an outfit gives a woman presence in any position, but don't overdo it with loud bracelets or rings on every finger. Avoid overly large or dangling earrings, which look unprofessional, in favor of button or small hoop styles. And again, select pieces in proportion to your size.

When accessorizing your ensembles, consider wearing a broach on your suit lapel or a silk square in the breast pocket to add pizzazz to your jacket. Tie a suit together with a belt at the waist. Add a scarf over the shoulder or around the neck to give that finishing touch. Take time to experiment with accessories. Perhaps you have a great wardrobe, but have you counted your accessories lately? Try accessorizing outfits in different ways to create new looks with the same pieces.

Hosiery accessorizes for less. Go with ultra-sheer varieties for just a hint of color. The rule of thumb for hosiery is that the color should match either the skirt or pant hem or the color of the shoe. Pass up black stockings in favor of off-black or charcoal-gray. Taupe is a good color; it goes with most everything in fall and winter wardrobes.

Unless you wear a white uniform, avoid white hosiery. (No one has white legs.) Go with an off-white, pearl, or mushroom color. A lot of women like to wear a black dress, white stockings, and black shoes. This kind of contrast actually makes you appear shorter and your legs wider. If you are tall and slim, then by all means, try it, but if you are petite or have large calves, don't.

Hairstyle. Your hairstyle should be a conservative cut that is easy to manage. A woman who is always fixing her hair is communicating that she is not interested in business. The style should not be too short or tailored, or long and overly feminine. If your hair is past your shoulder, pull it out of your face. Extremely long hair should be cut at least a couple of inches so there is less weight and better opportunity for curl.

When considering a hairstyle, seek professional advice. Get a haircut suitable for your face, personality, hair type, and career. Long straight hair parted in the middle is dated, and so is teased or "big" hair. Be sure to update your look periodically for something new and contemporary.

When it comes to color, again, seek the advice of a professional. Lightening your hair two or three shades softens facial lines. Or perhaps you would like to warm up your hair color with a touch of red. In any case, change the color gradually. If you choose to go gray, you may consider a rinse to enhance the shade. Be sure to modify your makeup and the clothing colors you wear around your face to accommodate the change.

The executive image includes makeup even if it's a little. Makeup gives a woman's face a finished look. While most men have good skin color, perhaps as a result of shaving and after-shave, women generally seem not to. Enhance your own good looks with a touch of blush, mascara and lip gloss. If you want to add more color, consider foundation and eye shadow. Good colors for eye shadow are teal, navy, deep violet, taupe, and brown. Avoid bright pinks, peaches, blues, and greens. Lipstick color should enhance your own lip color. If you like bright, deep reds save those for after work. A painted lady is not taken seriously in the office.

Another point about applying your makeup: blend it! Be particularly sensitive to blending foundation under the chin and toward the neck at the jaw line, as well as to blending eye colors and blush. Be sure to apply your makeup under plenty of lighting, since the light at work is probably strong. A rule of thumb about makeup—if the lip color, eye color, or blush jumps out at you when you give yourself the once-over before leaving, you have too much on. The same rule applies to fragrance—if you smell yourself, you have too much on. If you have a very strong perfume or cologne, you may consider going with eau de toilette or body splash, which are lighter in fragrance.

Nails are another part of the total image for women. You don't have to have long nails to keep them in good condition and looking great. Consider a weekly manicure for your nails' health, as well as a little something for yourself. Avoid extremely long nails and bright polish.

Personal hygiene is just as important for women as for men. Bathe every day, wear deodorant, and brush and floss your teeth. If you have apparent facial hair, bleach it. If your breath has a foul odor, it could be the sign of dental problems, so have your teeth cleaned and checked every six months. If your mouth tends to become dry, this too can result in bad breath. Drink fluids and chew a sugarless gum to moisten your mouth. Wash and condition your hair so it looks and feels healthy and shiny, and get it trimmed or shaped every six weeks.

Clean your face daily. Once or twice a week, use an exfoliating cleanser, a washcloth, or a buff pad and soap to remove dead skin cells and give your face a health glow.

EXERCISE

Examine your wardrobe. Check items to make sure they are clean and in good condition. List your professional wardrobe on the inventory that follows. Make sure to include accessories and shoes. What key pieces are needed to pull it together?

Business Wardrobe Inventory

Clothing Category   Color
Suits:...............................   ....
....
....

Sport coats/Blazers:...............   ....
....

Skirts/Trousers: ....
....
....

Skirts/Blouses: ....
....
....

Accessories
Shoes: ....
....
....

Hosiery/Socks: ....
....
....

Belts: ....
....
....

Scarves/Handkerchiefs: ....
....
....

Jewelry: ....
....
....

Miscellaneous: ....
....
....

After reviewing your business wardrobe inventory, consider other aspects of your total package. Does your hair, makeup, and so on send a consistent message?

EXERCISE

NINE

Business Casual

After learning how to dress for success in the 80s, the workforce is having to learn how to dress all over with "Business Casual." Business casual started showing up in the late 80s as women became more common in the workforce and successful as well. Women's entry into corporate America changed how men dressed for work and got the ball rolling for a new set of dress standards defined as Business Casual.

As baby boomers became CEOs they started incorporating a more relaxed attitude towards business dress such as the CEO of Apple and Microsoft. Further, as a way to improve employee morale and productivity during a period of intense downsizing, companies incorporated "Casual Fridays." Also, as a tip from successful Japanese companies where everyone from the CEO to the laborer wore the same outfit, introducing business casual was a way to make this hierarchy less visible and more participatory in management style.

Some other factors that have impacted business dress are computers and the Internet. Some advertisements even advocate individuals working at home conducting major business transactions in their pajamas via the Internet. Furthermore, as mentioned previously, the downsizing of America and high-tech capabilities have led many to open businesses out of their homes where ties and pantyhose are a thing of the past.

However, as much as business casual has been embraced, it has also been cause for concern and in some cases the extreme of business casual has resulted in disaster and elimination of the new policy. Many think that everyone and every company is "into" business casual and that it's "ok" to come to an interview in Dockers and a denim shirt. Wrong! It's also ok if you own the company to dress anyway you want, right? Wrong!

We know from previous chapters that most people form impressions based on limited information. Particularly in first time meetings, the limited information includes your dress. It is not suggested that we abolish business casual, but that it is interpreted correctly with positive rapport-building results rather than negative. Business casual is defined as relaxed clothing that is appropriate to conduct business in a professional manner.

IBM, notorious for strict dress guidelines that included white shirts and ties for men and skirted suits for women, has, over the years, succumbed to business casual as appropriate attire. Further, recent court decisions regarding women's right to wear pants have allowed women to get more relaxed in the workplace.

However, business casual is not always an appropriate manner to conduct business. In interviews, meetings with clients, and sales calls, dressing for success should not include casual attire. Yet on days when just working in the office, free from meetings and get togethers with clients, you might consider a relaxed version of business dress. A relaxed version, not your sweats or your favorite worn out jeans. Even for individuals in the travel business, although the industry does not dictate a suit and tie, that doesn't mean you have a green light to wear your most comfy of sweats or shorts.

The onset of business casual has spurred new lines of clothes, such as Levis Dockers for men and whole new clothing departments for women. There are also store consultants and personal shoppers to help you get relaxed at most upscale department stores such as Nordstroms. The Men's Warehouse, a nationwide off-priced retailer of men's wear advertises that their clothing consultants know just how to dress down your wardrobe.

Some companies such as banks, that allowed casual Fridays, are retracting it due to the poor manner in which it was interpreted. In this chapter the elements of business casual will be addressed with tips on how to dress down your current wardrobe without buying a whole new one.

As mentioned earlier, business casual is relaxed clothing that is appropriate to conduct business in a professional manner. For many, the interpretation has resulted in worn jeans, sandals, shorts, athletic shoes, strappy tops and sweats that could spell disaster for your career. Avoid your play clothing when putting together an ensemble for casual Friday. Consider instead good quality clothing in relaxed designs and fabrics. Lets focus on this more closely.

Business Casual for Men

Men have a lot of options for business casual. Whether in a white or blue-collar position, dressing casually should be a relaxed version of your regular attire. Depending on the nature of your business and where it is located, as well as the possibility of unplanned client interaction, your interpretation of business casual will vary. Here are some ideas for various types of professions.

Traditional Fields: Traditional professions include banking and finance, accounting, and law, and require the utmost in dress on a regular basis. But there is opportunity to get relaxed. Consider sport coats and blazers worn with tailored trousers and sport shirts, as well as relaxed styles of shoes such as loafers. Consider also a shirt and tie worn with a cardigan rather than a jacket. Choose belted pants with elastic in the waist for comfort as opposed to unbelted styles. Avoid baggy Dockers, jeans and athletic shoes. Also, avoid theme clothing such as your favorite western jacket and cowboy hat.

Fabrics should include wools and cottons blended with polyester, acrylic, silk, or linen. Avoid 100 percent polyester shirts that are shiny, with studs, fringe, or other decor. Choose plain colors or classic patterns such as glen, tartan and scotch plaids, and/or pin or chalk striped. This is not the time to wear the Hawaiian shirt you picked up in Maui this summer or that florescent colored shirt from the 70s. As well, avoid white pants and other resort apparel—save that for the cruise.

For variety in shirts, try mandarin or button-down collar styles. Sport shirts should be long sleeved for a finished appearance under a jacket. Another option might be a polo styled shirt worn with a blazer. This is the only time when a short sleeved shirt is appropriate.

Jewelry should be kept to a minimum with only a good watch and either a class ring or wedding ring. Avoid the earring in the ears even for casual day, as well as gold chains and bracelets.

Accessorize your business casual wardrobe as you would your regular work attire giving consideration to detail. Wear belts with conservative buckles, and socks that either match the color of your shoes or the color of your pants. Avoid white socks and bright argyles.

Bottom line, be on the safe side at work and have handy a blazer and trousers, or suit, white shirt, and tie just in case an unexpected appointment with a client arises. It's better to be safe than sorry.

Semitraditional Fields: Semitraditional fields include marketing and sales, high-tech, real estate, and education. Regularly, business attire includes more options than traditional fields and for casual days as well. Again, depending on the corporate climate, where you live, and the opportunity for client interaction, dressing casually allows you the opportunity to leave the suit and tie behind. Consider tailored Dockers and a sport shirt or polo styled shirt. Introduce denim shirts and cardigans, turtle or mock turtleneck pullovers, crew neck and v-neck sweaters. Consider deck or boat shoes for comfort. Button-down collars or mandarin styles in linen, cotton, or raw silk are great additions to casual days. For chilly days consider tweed or herringbone sport coats and cardigans over shirts.

For colors, choose the neutrals such as olive, gray, and black worn with splashes of plum, burgundy, mustard, teal, or brown. Consider prints in plaids and subdued florals, and trousers. Try suspenders with a long sleeve sport shirt in a tartan plaid or stripe and pleated trousers. Avoid bright greens and instead focus on forest or hunter greens in jackets and other items.

In semitraditional fields jeans are also appropriate for casual days but purchase tailored denim styles that are kept in tip top condition. Avoid your faded Levis 501's, baggy or oversized styles. Consider black, indigo, or khaki colors for jeans as opposed to teals, rusts, and whites.

Accessorize your casual outfit with the same attention to detail as your regular business attire. Avoid excessive jewelry. Again, a good watch and either a class ring or wedding ring are appropriate. Avoid white socks and focus on colors that either match your pants or shoes. Avoid white shoes and athletic styles. A good boat style is comfortable and spells business in a more relaxed manner. As well, avoid wearing hats to the office except to cover up when outside in the cold. Wear either a belt or suspenders (but not both) that are toned down yet interesting, such as braided leather suspenders. Further, when it comes to suspenders choose styles that attach to the inside button of your trousers rather than clip-on styles.

As well, like your regular business attire your relaxed styles should be in tip top condition and good quality. Make sure your clothes are clean and pressed with no stains or fraying seams. And just as a precaution, keep a blazer, shirt, and tie handy just in case the unexpected happens.

Creative Fields: Such fields include acting, fashion, advertising, interior design, art, and music. Again, depending on the corporate climate, where you live, and your particular job responsibilities, your casual attire will vary. Often advertising is classified as a creative field and hence, most people assume that gives them the right to wear the most avant-garde attire. However, advertising includes positions such as account executive and account VP, which are more like a semitraditional profession in scope, and art directors, which exemplify creative fields. So before kicking up your heels and yahooing the fact that you can wear anything on casual days, evaluate what others are wearing and what your job responsibilities include. If interaction with clients is part of the job description you might want to tone down a bit. But here are some ideas for those in the creative fields that still have to communicate business with style on a daily basis.

Consider structured or unstructured sport coats with plain T-shirts and nice jeans. As well, jeans and denim shirts or turtlenecks is another alternative. Avoid T-shirts with messages and holes, rather have a collection in a variety of colors that are worn for work only. Consider flannel shirts with trousers or jeans, or crewneck sweaters and pants as relaxed alternatives.

How about leather as in leather pants, vests, hats, and so forth? Consider wearing one piece at a time rather than dressing like your local Harley Club. Avoid hats at work at all costs. You may consider a leather or cloth vest worn with a colorful shirt and pants; however, it is important that the colors coordinate. Avoid bright colors such as pink, bright purple, and fluorescent. You might choose to wear that Hawaiian shirt with a pair of solid colored fitted jeans that match tucked in or worn out.

Regarding accessories, they are just as important in the creative fields as they are in traditional ones. Since your clothing communicates in part your creative abilities, consider interesting accessories such as belts, scarves, pocket squares, and jewelry. Yes, you can wear your earring just forget the nose, eyebrow, tongue, and chin rings. Shoes can include athletic styles that are clean and in good condition. Try also deck or boat styles or soft Italian slip ons.

For men, dressing casually for work suggests dressing professionally yet comfortably. Be on top of your personal hygiene, hair style, nails, and teeth. Make sure that your wardrobe is clean and pressed, fits properly and is in good condition and you will be just right for business and comfortable too.

Business Casual for Women

When women entered the workforce in the 70s they mimicked men in their dress. As they became more successful and confident they developed their own style that spelled business yet femininity as well. This change led to more relaxed attitudes toward business attire, which in turn helped get the ball rolling for business casual. However, women, like men, went to the extreme when it came to casual Fridays because of lack of direction of what business casual really meant. Like men, women are employed in traditional, semitraditional, and creative positions. And depending on the corporate climate and where they live appropriate business casual varies.

Traditional fields: Traditional fields include banking and finance, accounting, and law. For women employed in these fields business casual suggests pant suits and separates rather than dresses and skirted suits. Consider a cardigan rather than a blazer or perhaps a sport coat paired up with tailored trousers. Shirts and blouses can be long or short sleeved in silk, cotton, or polyester but avoid sleeveless, halter, and tank tops. Jackets can be single or double breasted, with a collar or without, short or long, in wool, raw silk, and/or linen. However, do make sure that the jacket is tailored and lined for a finished appearance. Try a turtle or mock turtleneck with pants and blazer or a sweater worn with a blazer.

Pants should be tailored style and pleated for comfort. Consider styles with belt loops and a fly front with or without cuffs. Avoid bell bottoms and harem pants and go for flared or straight leg styles. Try two piece silk outfits in either a skirt or pant with a jacket.

Accessorize outfits with belts, scarves, pocket squares, jewelry, and shoes. Don't forget hosiery—it is a must whether you are wearing pants or skirt at any length. Avoid excessively designed jewelry and belts and rather maintain a conservative approach to these pieces. Jewelry should be either gold, silver, or pearls. Consider shoes in a loafer style with an inch or 3/4 inch heel to wear with your tailored separates. Avoid sandals and athletic shoes at all costs.

Colors for your business casual wardrobe should revolve around the neutrals such as olive, navy, black, and winter white. Avoid white and save that for your next vacation. Consider knits as opposed to woven pieces; however, make sure they are knits with lots of body. Jersey or single knits are too revealing and too casual.

Semitraditional fields: Semitraditional fields include education, marketing, sales, real estate, and high-tech occupations. Here, your options for business casual are greater than traditional fields but not to the extreme of creative ones. Consider tailored trousers with blouses and cardigans or blazers. As well, consider city shorts worn with cardigans or a blazer and top. Avoid leggings or stirrup pants of any kind! City shorts, unlike regular shorts, can be cuffed or uncuffed and land about two to three inches above the knee. You may choose to wear knee high hosiery in conservative designs with loafers or regular panty hose with low-heeled pumps. Consider vests as another option along with cotton twill tailored trousers. Turtle or mock turtleneck pullovers or polo styled tops worn with a blazer are comfortable but spell professional as well. Try crew and V-neck sweaters in wools, cotton, or acrylic worn with corduroy pants, skirts, split skirts, or city shorts. Do not wear plunging necklines, short or midriff tops.

Build your business casual wardrobe around the colors that are most predominate in your existing wardrobe such as navy, black, teal, olive, gray, and taupe. Avoid excessive use of pastels as well as bright colors. Also, choose more tailored styles for your business casual wardrobe rather than ruffles, lace, chiffons, and flowers. It's okay to have flower patterns; however, your Sunday best is not appropriate for work whether it's casual Friday or not. Also, avoid see-through fabrics—wear those on your own time. Consider wearing denim in tailored jeans, shirts, skirts, or dresses. Don't wear your faded 501s or your cargo pants.

Remember to accessorize with scarves, belts, jewelry, pocket squares, hosiery, and other items but don't overdo it. One set of earrings is the limit. Shoes can include boat or deck shoes as well as loafers and slip ons. Avoid hats and themed apparel such as western wear. Remember, too many accessories add confusion.

Creative fields: Creative fields include interior design, fashion, acting, music, art, and advertising. As mentioned previously, the advertising field includes positions such as account executive that deal consistently with clients. Art directors deal with the artistic aspects of advertising. For those who are account executives you may want to dress more conservatively than your creative partners. Building rapport is essential with a client and being the utmost in creativity in your business casual is not what they are expecting from you. However, you do have the opportunity to incorporate more fashion-forward pieces in your business casual wardrobe than those in traditional and semitraditional fields.

Consider plain T-shirts worn with blazers, classic Keds, and nice jeans. Try a simple white shirt with jeans and a sweater tied around the neck. You might consider silk or polyester tops and bottoms worn with interesting accessories and a vest. Try flat sandals or open-toed shoes in colors that coordinate with your outfit. Avoid skimmers. Try stirrup pants with an interesting sweater or top (only if you have the body to get away with it).

As an individual employed in a creative field, your choices should take into account current fashion trends and the fact that people expect you to be creative in your dress; however, don't be a prisoner to fashion. Incorporate key pieces that will update your wardrobe. Try interesting fabrics and patterns, avoiding translucent or revealing types. Again, no plunging necklines, midriff, halter, or sleeveless tops. As well, don't wear evening clothes such as the slip dress to work. It doesn't spell casual and definitely not business.

Make sure to accessorize your clothing ensemble with interesting pieces. Earrings should be kept to one pair but can include interesting shapes and colors. Avoid the nose, eyebrow, tongue, and chin rings. Also, business casual is not the time to wear rings on every finger, ankle bracelets, and noisy bracelets. Save these for your time.

When dressing for business casual, you have the opportunity to be professional but comfortable at the same time. However, don't forget to practice personal hygiene, wear a moderate amount of makeup, and have your hair styled neatly. This is not the time to put sparkles in your hair, color it temporarily blue, orange, or green, or wear it with enough gel that it stands straight up. Further, avoid wearing your favorite perfume or your black nail polish and save those for your time.

Also, it is important that your clothing is in tip-top condition and is clean and pressed. As well, be sure that what you wear fits. Tight jeans and tops don't look good on anyone whether for casual Fridays or not. Further, you will note that I did not mention the appropriateness of sweats or athletic shoes for business casual. Work is not the place for either of them.

Today, business casual is part of many corporations, dress policies such as IBM, Hewlett Packard, and Dupont. However, many individuals are ruining their chances for promotion by taking it to the extreme. Whether going on an interview or dealing with clients, dress for success; however, on those days when the agenda doesn't include important meetings, dress comfortably but still professional. It enhances rapport among peers and subordinates yet still communicates that you know what you're doing.

EXERCISE

Evaluate your company's corporate climate, where you live, and current dress policies. Is business casual an accepted practice for employees? If so, examine your current wardrobe and determine the key pieces that will create a casual but professionally minded attire for your job and company.

TEN

After Five

The executive image doesn't stop when the clock hits five. Frankly, the impression you make on others after work is just as, if not more, important than the one you make between nine and five. Whether for a black tie affair, a company picnic, a movie with colleagues, or dinner with clients, dressing well is a must.

For both men and women dressing for business-related activities has many options, but it starts with the basics:

- Organize your after-five wardrobe as you did your professional one. Order shirts by color from light to dark, with long and short sleeves in separate groups. Organize sweaters, blazers, pants, and skirts in the same way.
- This wardrobe can be as individualized as well, so make the most of the clothes you wear by tying them together with scarves, belts, and ties.
- Fit is just as important in your after-five attire as it is at work. Tight or ill-fitting clothing draws attention to figure problems.
- Select a color scheme for your wardrobe. After organizing your closet, you'll begin to see the colors that you are attracted to. Build around one or several of the neutrals—navy, black, gray, olive, camel, ivory, and white.
- Keep your casual, after-five attire in tip-top condition.

Dressing for special occasions has guidelines all its own. Here are some tips for avoiding the embarrassment of showing up under or overdressed for the occasion.

- When the invitation says "casual," it's best to call your hosts and ask them what they mean. Sometimes "casual" means slacks and a top, sometimes a sport coat and tie or a cocktail dress. The type of affair, the region of the country, and the people present will have a lot to do with dress requirements. If the affair is an open house it probably calls for a suit or a sport coat and tie for men, a dress, two-piece dress, jacket and city shorts, or, depending on the time of the day, dinner suit or cocktail dress for women.

  Remember, the term "casual" has different meanings for different parts of the country. East coast dress tends to be more formal than that of the middle and western regions. The term "casual" also implies more formal attire in large cities than in small towns.

  The important thing to remember when attending any function, whether it calls for jeans or a sport coat and tie, is to look your best. Clean and press your best jeans. Don't think "casual" means "sloppy."

- For a breakfast, lunch, or early cocktail party, consider these alternatives. Women—A dress or suit in linen (for summer), silk, cotton, or wool, with pumps or sling backs—not strippy evening sandals. Men—A dark suit, or a sport coat with coordinating trousers, dress shirt, tie, and polished shoes.

- For an evening function, with cocktails at six or dinner at seven, consider these options. Women—A black or dark-colored dress or a black or dark-colored evening suit, ultra-sheer hosiery in dark tones, evening pumps or strapped sandals, dramatic jewelry, and a small handbag or clutch. Velvet is worn around the Christmas season. Men—A dark suit in navy, black, or charcoal gray, tie, dress shirt in white or colored with contrasting white collar, and black shoes.

- For a black tie affair, consider the following: Women—Short, three quarter, or long evening dress in silk, chiffon, crepe, taffeta, or organza (velvet should be confined to the holiday season or during the cooler months from October through January); dramatic jewelry, evening clutch, strapped evening sandals, and ultra-sheer hosiery. Men—Black-tie tuxedo, dress shirt, black hose, and black patent leather shoes. As an executive, you don't want to overdo it. Women should avoid overly bright, flamboyant colors and designs, and men should avoid fur lined cummerbunds and extravagant ties. Stick to the basic black.

■ For a formal affair such as a ball, consider these options. Women—A long gown (no pants), with or without sequins, in taffeta, silk, chiffon, or organza, with dramatic jewelry, clutch, strapped sandals, and ultra-sheer hosiery. Men—White tie and tailcoat. Black tuxedo is acceptable. Again, don't overdo it.

Some Basics After Five for Men

■ Khaki slacks in fine cotton twills, double pleated or plain in front. These go with anything all year long. You might also consider pants in an olive cotton twill to mix and match with your casual wardrobe.

■ Crewneck or V-neck sweaters in cotton, acrylic, or wool in classic colors such as hunter green, navy, camel, and gray. A soft yellow is also acceptable. Avoid baby blue.

■ Tartan plaid shirts in blue, green, red, and navy combinations. Button-down pinpoint oxford shirts in white, light blue, pink, gray, yellow, and off-white (for some complexions) complete a shirt collection for outside the office. Try turtlenecks or mock turtlenecks in a fine interlock knit for an alternative. No color restrictions apply.

■ Polo-styled shirts, long or short-sleeved in a fine interlock knit, work in any color. If you choose 100 percent cotton, take the shrink factor into account. You may have to get a size larger.

■ Slacks, in pinwale cotton corduroy or tropical-weight wool gabardine styles, in navy, charcoal gray, black, and brown.

■ Walking shorts in wardrobe neutrals, with or without cuffs.

■ Sport coats and blazers in navy or camel, or in black or brown tweed. Also consider linen and raw silk sport coats and blazers in wheat, off-white, and muted patterns.

- Jeans—dressed-up styles for various occasions. They should be commercially laundered and starched or washed and starched at home for a crisp look. When they start to fade or appear worn, stop wearing them.

- Cordovan, camel, or brown loafers (with or without the tassels), dock shoes, and sneakers (not high tops).

- Avoid bright yellow, light or sky blue, purple, and orange in favor of navy blue, white, maroon, khaki, beige, and olive.

- Good-quality leather is just as important in shoes and belts after five as it is during business hours. Avoid cheap leather and vinyl.

- Look for blends of 50, 60, or 65 percent natural fiber and 35, 40, or 50 percent synthetic. These give the look of natural fiber with the ease of care provided by synthetic. Exceptions may be made when you are purchasing ski wear and some athletic apparel.

Some Basics After Five for Women

- Khaki skirts and pants in fine cotton twills or wool gabardines.

- Tropical-weight wool gabardine trousers in wardrobe neutrals such as navy, black, olive, camel, winter-white, and gray.

- Cotton broadcloth, pinpoint oxford shirts, or silk blouses, either long or short-sleeved, in complimentary colors suited to your complexion and wardrobe. Stripes and patterns add variety, as do camp-styled or oversize shirts in rayon and silk.

- Denim pants and skirts. Pants should be laundered commercially with starch or starched at home for a crisp look. When they start to fade, stop wearing them. Don't buy prewashed or faded styles.

- Jackets and blazers in navy, black or brown tweed, burgundy, camel, or natural in linen, raw silk, and wool gabardine or flannel to top skirts, trousers, jeans, and shorts.

- Turtleneck or mock turtlenecks in fine interlock knits in colors complimentary to your wardrobe and complexion.

- Polo-styled shirts, long and short-sleeved, in a fine interlock. If the shirt is 100 percent cotton, take the shrink factor into account when buying. You may have to buy a size larger.

- Walking shorts in wardrobe neutrals and in classic houndstooth, tweeds, and muted plaids. Choose wool gabardines, wool flannels, linen, rayon/wool blends, and fine cotton twills.
- Sneakers, leather flats—either loafer or skimmer styles—and sandals. Consider loafers with a moderate heel for in-between occasions.
- A leather handbag in a wardrobe neutral. The neutral most prominent in your wardrobe will be the best color for your bag.
- For dinner, theater, or the symphony, a simple, black, shift-style cocktail dress or a dinner suit dressed up with dazzling jewelry and other accessories.
- Earrings, pendants, and chains in gold, silver, or pearls.
- Good-quality leather. Avoid cheap leather and vinyl.
- Look for blends of 50, 60, or 65 percent natural fiber and 35, 40, or 50 percent synthetic for the comfort and look of a natural fiber with the ease of care of a synthetic.

EXERCISE

Organize your casual wardrobe in a fashion similar to your professional wardrobe. Give a simple description of each item, like "V-neck sweater," when jotting down what you have. Use the chart below. After completing the chart, make notes of which items will pull it all together.

Clothing Item   Color

Jackets: ....

....

Shirts/blouses

Short-sleeved solid: ....

....

....

Short-sleeved patterned: ....

....

....

EXERCISE

EXERCISE

Long-sleeved solid: ....
....
....

Long-sleeved patterned: ....
....
....

Sweaters: ....
....
....

Trousers: ....
....
....

Skirts: ....
....
....

Shorts: ....
....
....

Shoes: ....
....
....

Jewelry: ....
....
....

Miscellaneous: ....
....
....

Now list the items that will pull this wardrobe together.

1. .... 6. ....

2. .... 7. ....

3. .... 8. ....

4. .... 9. ....

5. .... 10. ....

EXERCISE

ELEVEN

Accessorizing the Executive Image

Accessories

Most cakes need frosting, and most ensembles need accessorizing. Those fine details are the finishing touches on your executive image.

A basic list of men's and women's accessories has been included in an earlier chapter. Now let's take a closer look at accessories and how to use them.

For Women:

- Scarves. Scarves can be tied in various ways around the neck or at the waist. Around-the-neck scarves can be tied in an ascot, necktie, scout, fan, classic square, or twist fashion.

    For an ascot, take a medium-sized square scarf, open it, then grasp the center, tying a knot. Turn it inside out so that the knot doesn't show, then take the opposite corners around your neck, tying them in back. Tuck the front into your collar.

    For the necktie, take an oblong scarf and, starting from the front of the neck, wrap the ends around the neck twice so that both ends are in front. Then tie the scarf once, allowing the ends to drape over one another.

    For the scout, take a medium-sized square scarf and fold the opposite ends together so that it forms a triangle. Drape the longest edge around your neck so that the top of the triangle is pointing down the back. Tie the ends once or twice, forming a knot. If you like, the point can be placed in the front or over the shoulder.

For the fan, take a medium or large square scarf and fold it in a back and forth fashion, like an accordion. Holding the ends, wrap the scarf around the neck once and tie it once in front. Fluff the ends so that the fan drapes in the center, or, if you like, to the side.

For the classic square, take a medium or large square scarf and fold it so that it is oblong. Wrap it around the neck once, tying it in a knot. Let the ends drape in front or to the side.

For the twist, knot the ends of an oblong scarf. Now twist it so it looks like a rope. Wrap it twice around the neck, tucking the ends into the scarf.

An alternative to scarves are pocket squares in silk prints or lace, to add that extra something to a suit jacket or blazer. Stuff the square in the breast pocket, allowing the points to show one to two inches, or fold the square or stuff it in the pocket *hiding* the points. Scarves should be silk or wool. Pocket squares can be silk, wool, or cotton. Unless you can find fine, fluid polyester, avoid synthetics.

- Stockings are an inexpensive accessory that can update almost any item of apparel for the upcoming season. Use them to bring out hidden colors in dresses and skirts. Avoid textured stockings in favor of ultra-sheer varieties. Remember, the stockings should match the shoe, skirt, dress, or pant. If you plan to go with a color, try ultra-sheer shades instead of opaque.

  If you enjoy the look of light-colored hose, choose off-white, pearl, or mushroom sheers; avoid white. Don't forget that contrasting hose in light shades makes you appear shorter and your legs appear larger.

  Navy is a hard color to match, so consider an ultra-sheer black or charcoal gray instead. This will give the appearance of navy without the disadvantages. If you have any doubts about what color hose to wear, stick with skin-toned hosiery.

- Hats, once a must at every occasion, are now seldom seen and are generally inappropriate for the aspiring present-day executive.

- Belts probably offer the greatest possibilities for spicing up a wardrobe. There is such a variety to choose from: double-wrap, fabric, chain, cinch, leather, wide, thin, dull, and glittery. Consider a contrastingly colored belt with a solid color dress. An unstructured blazer can be closed and belted for a new look.

Try a different belt than the one that came with the garment. You might even consider eliminating the threaded belt loops on the side seams so belts can be interchanged easily.

Complete your suit with a belt either in the same color as the suit or in a contrasting color. For example, put a brown faux crocodile belt with a navy suit. For a black or red suit, use a black belt. The black belt with the red suit should be matched with black pumps. Add some excitement to a skirt and blouse or a two-piece dress by adding a belt, in the same or in a contrasting color, with an interesting buckle.

■ Jewelry makes a strong impact with any outfit. Pendants or brooches sparkle up a blazer lapel or add pizzazz to a collarless jacket. Earrings are a must, to give shine to a woman's face. In selecting your jewelry, choose gold or silver tones or pearls, or colored stones in black, blue, and red surrounded by gold or silver, to accessorize with color. Avoid plastic and wood pieces, and stay away from dangling earrings, multiple rings, and noisy bracelets. Choose button or small hoop earrings in proportion to your size. Include in your collection medium to large necklaces in choker and longer lengths for accessorizing different ensembles.

■ Handbags are basic to any outfit. Choose one versatile enough that you won't have to change bags with every outfit. Go with the most prominent neutral in your wardrobe, but avoid white and beige; these tend to soil quickly. Consider a bag in a cordovan (burgundy) color, since it goes with most outfits.

The bag should be of good-quality leather, not plastic or vinyl. It should be in proportion to your size and not so large that you can't find anything in it. You may wish to try a shoulder bag for ease of carrying when your hands are occupied—say, with your briefcase. But if you have large hips, you may want to avoid this style altogether, since it adds greater width in that area. Choose tailored styles with minimal detailing. You might want to consider some with gold closures or similar accents.

- Shoes should be pumps, with heels ranging from one to two-and-a-half inches, and styles should be on the conservative side. Spectator pumps are great for some classic excitement. Spectators come in a variety of contrasting shades, including white and black, white and navy, white and red, camel and black, and beige and white.

    Remember, comfort is essential. *Don't* buy shoes that hurt.

    Avoid white shoes in favor of a light taupe or beige. If you wear bright shoes, the bright color must be repeated somewhere else, preferably near the face in a scarf or blouse.

- Glasses are now considered accessories. Research has shown that women are perceived as more intelligent with glasses than without.

    Frames should softly follow the shape of the face without emphasizing facial contour. If your face is round, round glasses will only accentuate the roundness.

    Make sure that the frames you choose do not go too far down your cheeks and that the top of the frames is even with your eyebrows. The width of the frames should be the same as the temples.

    If you want shaded lenses, go with a 5 to 10 percent tint in the same color as your eyes. Avoid overly flamboyant styles and colors for traditional fields and conservative companies. Choose tortoise, black, deep purple, burgundy, navy, wires, or frameless. In creative or glamour fields, however, drama is expected.

- A briefcase or attaché case is a must. Most department stores and leather shops offer two sizes of attaché cases, one for women and one for men. Women's styles are often sleeker and smaller in design than men's. Choose black, brown, or cordovan cases with minimal decoration.

Some other tips:

- Don't overdo it. Accessories used in moderation add glamour; too many add confusion.
- When accessorizing with gold and silver jewelry, stick with one or the other. If you are wearing gold earrings, wear a belt with a gold buckle and a necklace or pendant in gold.

- Print scarves are a good bet for any outfit, even print or patterned outfits. Top a print skirt with a solid blouse and wear a scarf that includes colors from the skirt.
- Be sure to keep your figure proportions in mind when accessorizing. If you have large hips, wearing a cinch belt will certainly make your hips appear larger. If you're full-figured, try a belt in the same color, as opposed to a contrasting color.
- Make use of various sizes and shapes of scarves. Oblong scarves are ideal for cummerbund effects around the waist.

For Men:

- Socks for men are like hosiery for women; they are an essential component of a man's wardrobe. Now fashion has entered the picture, with patterns and prints.

  Socks should match the color either of the shoe or of the trouser leg. Avoid bright argyles and go with subtle patterns in muted shades. You don't want to call attention to your feet. Moreover, your hosiery should be able to stay up comfortably around the midcalf of the leg or knee. (A hairy leg is not a pretty sight!)

  Belts should be a high-quality leather in black, brown, camel, or cordovan. You will want the color of the belt to match your shoes. The buckle should be conservative, refined, preferably square and an inch to an inch-and-a-half in width. Cordovan-colored (that is, burgundy-colored) belts go with most suit colors. For formal occasions where a suit is called for, wear a black belt and shoes with a dark-colored suit.

- Suspenders are now an option for today's executive. Notice what your superiors or colleagues wear before going all out with them. If you do wear suspenders, consider subtle colors and prints for traditional professions and companies and brights for creative and glamour fields. Your trousers will have a button on the inside of the pant waist to attach the suspenders.

- Jewelry should be minimal. About the only jewelry you'll need is a classic watch, and a wedding ring if you are married. Diamond jewelry and gold chains are not appropriate. Collar pins give a refined look to shirts and add polish to a dress shirt. Tie clips and pins are rarely seen nowadays.

    Lapel pins and insignia rings should only be worn if you are sure they are sending a friendly or positive message. Avoid wearing ID bracelets, except for medical reasons. Cufflinks should be classically styled, simple, and discreet in size. Consider gold, silver, or stone cufflinks only.

- Attaché or briefcases are a necessary part of a man's wardrobe. Choose a leather case in cordovan, brown, or black. The style should be plain, classically simple, and functional.

- Glasses can add to or detract from your appearance. Frames should pick up the color from the hair. Heavier-built men should wear heavier frames. Whether you choose wire, plastic, or frameless glasses, choose a style that complements your facial contour. If your face is round, choose angular frames or lenses. Choose from tortoise, navy, gray, or black when selecting colors.

- A great deal has already been said about buying ties, but little about knotting them. Rule of thumb: the smaller the knot, the more formal and affluent the message. Common knotting methods include the Windsor, the half Windsor, and the four-in-hand knot. Check for a tab on the back of the large end of the tie. The tab allows the small end of the tie to be slipped through so it doesn't show.

- Handkerchiefs should be cotton, linen, or silk. Cotton or linen handkerchiefs should be white, while silk handkerchiefs can be muted patterns in burgundy, teal, navy, red, brown, yellow, beige, or forest green. Patterned silk handkerchiefs coordinate well with tweed and herringbone jackets but also give pizzazz to a navy, glen plaid, and gray suit as well as blazers and sport jackets. Patterned silk handkerchiefs needn't match the tie but should share some colors. White handkerchiefs are better with navy and other dark-colored suits and blazers.

■ Shoes for men should include loafers (slip-ons) and "ties," otherwise known as oxfords. Colors should include black, brown, or cordovan. Shoe color should match belt color.

Underneath It All

Undergarments serve the function of camouflaging and supporting the body. Slips for women and undershirts for men camouflage the body when sheer fabrics are worn. This is an important function in projecting the executive image.

Some foundation garments are designed to offer support, to hide, to reproportion, and to accentuate certain areas of the body. Others are designed to appeal to the sexy side of a woman's or man's nature. Today, through technological advancements in fabrics and construction, women can have it all—and so can men!

For Women:

■ If you are full or large-busted, purchase bras that give plenty of support. The bra manufacturer Bali recognizes that women can be small, average, or full-busted, yet wear the same bra size. Some sexy bras provide little support and therefore are not advisable for fuller busts. Consider bras with underwire supports and thicker adjustable straps.

    An alternative to bras to support the full bust are minimizer bras, which minimize the largeness of the breasts. If you are small-busted, you can wear bras that do not have underwire supports or padded bras. However, no matter what your age or cup size, it is important to provide support to the breast tissue.

■ Avoid girdles. Instead, exercise, maintain your ideal weight, and keep physically fit. Girdles used to be worn not only to firm things up but to hold up stockings, until it was learned that they inhibit circulation. If you want the appearance of a smooth, firm line, choose support or control top pantyhose or control panties. They don't constrict the body as much as girdles.

- Choose undergarments in neutral, peach, pink, champagne, or skin tones. White undergarments don't even approach most skin tones, and are therefore likely to show through. Choose camisoles in beige, champagne, peach, or pink shades to wear with translucent tops.

- Purchase bras that accommodate different necklines, including halter tops and strapless garments. Going braless is *not* part of the executive image! Purchase slips to accommodate different hem lengths, slits, and hemlines. Tack back the corners of slips with slits so that the slits are triangular-shaped; then the slip won't show.

- If you want to wear deep-colored lingerie, such as navy, black, red, violet, or green, make sure that the garment is completely opaque. Wearing blue undergarments under white is inappropriate.

- When wearing a translucent dress, wear a full slip or a combination of a camisole and slip.

- Wear bikini and hipster panties with caution. Briefs or panties should not create indentations that will be seen through the pants. Again, use color with caution, making sure your panties don't show through. Get panties with a cotton crotch. Cotton breathes and helps to keep the body dry, lowering the possibility of yeast infections. An alternative to wearing briefs with pantyhose are Underalls or pantyhose with a cotton crotch. This gives a smooth appearance to your ensembles.

- When purchasing undergarments, give particular consideration to fit. To determine cup size for bras, measure yourself with a tape measure first around the rib cage right underneath the breasts, then around the middle of the breasts across the nipple. The difference between these two measurements will determine your cup size. A one-inch difference is a size A, two inches is a B, three inches is a C, four inches is a D, and a five-inch difference is a size E. Check to make sure that the middle of the front of the bra lies comfortably on the sternum bone. The bra should fasten comfortably on the middle hooks. Finally, purchase bras that hold your breasts in place and conceal your nipples.

  If you need a custom bra or have had a mastectomy and need a prosthesis, Cameo Coutures, a Dallas-based firm, is one place to look. Sears also offers prostheses through their catalog.

■ Panties should not be constricting and tight. If they start riding up, they're too small.

For Men:

Men's undergarments are just as varied today as women's.

■ It's important to wear an undershirt with dress shirts. When the shirt is closed and worn with a tie, choose a crewneck style; when worn open, wear a v-neck style. In any case, the undershirt should not show when the shirt is opened at the top.

■ Men's underwear comes in a variety of styles, materials, and colors. It includes regular, hipster, bikini briefs, boxers, and tapered boxer shorts. Tapered boxers are cut slimmer in the leg than regular boxers. Choose a style comfortable for you, but be sure, if you choose bikini or hipster briefs, that lines don't show through the pants.

■ If you choose colored undergarments, be sure that the colors don't show through.

■ If you choose synthetic briefs, make sure they have a cotton crotch to keep that area dry.

EXERCISE

Take an inventory of your accessories. Are there any you are missing? Below are two charts, one for women and one for men. List the pieces you have in each category and give a brief description, including the color, pattern, material, and style. Also note the possibilities for each piece. For example: "Pendant: Silver `S'-shaped, medium-size; for navy and winter-white jacket lapels, gray and plaid collarless suit jackets, purple and black dresses." "Tie: regimental stripe, red and blue; for gray suit, navy blazer, white shirt, and khaki pants." Once you've complete your inventory, reread the section on accessories and identify the pieces that will pull your executive image together.

EXERCISE

EXERCISE

Accessory Inventory for Women

Accessory Category	Description	Goes With

Scarves:

.... | .... | ....
.... | .... | ....
.... | .... | ....

Belts:

.... | .... | ....
.... | .... | ....
.... | .... | ....

Jewelry:

.... | .... | ....
.... | .... | ....
.... | .... | ....

Necklaces:

.... | .... | ....
.... | .... | ....
.... | .... | ....

Pendants:

.... | .... | ....
.... | .... | ....
.... | .... | ....

Bracelets:

.... | .... | ....
.... | .... | ....
.... | .... | ....

Earrings:

.... | .... | ....
.... | .... | ....

Accessory Category	Description	Goes With
Hosiery:		
....	....	....
....	....	....
....	....	....
	....	
Shoes:		
....	....	....
....	....	....
....	....	....
	....	
Handbags:		
....	....	....
....	....	....
....	....	....
	....	
Attaché cases:		
....	....	....
....	....	....
....	....	....
	....	
Miscellaneous:		
....	....	....
....	....	....
....	....	....

EXERCISE

Accessories that will enhance my current wardrobe:

1. .... 6. ....
2. .... 7. ....
3. .... 8. ....
4. .... 9. ....
5. .... 10. ....

EXERCISE

Accessory Inventory for Men

Accessory Category	Description	Goes With

Ties:

....
....
....

Belts:

....
....
....

Handkerchiefs Cotton/Linen:

....
....
....

Silk:

....
....
....

Jewelry:

....
....
....

Socks:

....
....

Shoes:

....

Accessory Category	Description	Goes With
Attaché cases:		
....	....	....
....	....	....
....	....	....
Miscellaneous:		
....	....	....
....	....	....
....	....	....

Accessories that will enhance my current wardrobe:

1. ....   6. ....
2. ....   7. ....
3. ....   8. ....
4. ....   9. ....
5. ....   10. ....

EXERCISE

TWELVE

Business Travel

A re you the kind of traveler who wants to take *everything*, wherever you go? Do you face the same dilemma every time you pack, how you can be sure to take along the right attire for every event on your agenda? Fret no more! You can become a smart traveler with just a little careful planning.

In most professions travel is part of the job description. This means more than extra meetings. Whether you are attending an association conference, servicing a client, or prospecting, social functions like banquets and cocktail parties may well be part of the evening's agenda during your trip and must be taken into account when you are deciding what to pack. The length of your trip is another important consideration. Above all, you must be equipped to project an executive image no matter where your travels take you.

Already prepared to take a steamer trunk for that three-day trip? Keep it in the attic. With a little planning you can probably carry all you need in a garment bag—and still look your best.

Basic Travel Tips

Because you may need to dress for a variety of occasions, the first thing you want to aim for in a travel wardrobe is versatility. It should not be necessary, for example, to change into another outfit for the evening. Men, if you're wearing a suit, stay in it; you can change your shirt or tie, if you prefer. Women could wear a blazer and dress combination for day activities, then remove the blazer and add dramatic jewelry for evening pizzazz!

Here are a few other mainstays.

■ To accommodate any weather condition you may encounter, bring an all-weather coat, a raincoat with a zip-in lining to provide warmth in cooler climates. The fabric of the outercoat is usually a poplin or gabardine weave, providing a windbreaker for breezy weather conditions. London Fog, Misty Harbor, and Burberry are reliable brands in all-weather coats. For added protection slip a folding umbrella into your briefcase.

■ Pick up toilet articles such as after-shave, aspirin, lotion, perfume, cleanser, and deodorant in trial sizes to minimize bulk. In fact, sample perfumes and colognes in small tubes are excellent for traveling with variety but not bulk. Hairdryers, irons, and contact lens heating units are also available in portable travel sizes. All can be purchased at your local grocery, discount, or drug store.

■ If you're traveling overseas, make sure your electrical appliances can adapt to overseas voltages. Invest in an adapter unit if you are unsure. You will probably also need a package of plug adapters to accommodate the different kinds of outlets found overseas. These electrical adapter units can be purchased at your local hardware or electronics stores.

■ Consider garment items made predominantly of natural fibers like wool, silk, and cotton. Wrinkles can be easily steamed out of these clothes by hanging them in the bathroom when you take a shower.

■ If you're not staying in a hotel where wake-up calls are an available service (or are unsure about this), consider bringing a portable alarm clock. Another alternative is a wristwatch equipped with an alarm mode.

■ Invest in a good garment bag or a suitcase with a pulley in a size 20-to-24 inch. This is still large enough to put all your necessities for your trip but small enough to take on board. Either with a garment bag or a pullman, choose one of nylon or polyester with lots of compartments.

- Combining outfits on hangers will save room in garment bags. Shirt, pants, and jacket can all go on one hanger. You can also buy multi-purpose hangers that hold more than one skirt or pair of pants. Hook and drape belts, scarves, and neckties onto hangers as well.

- Whether you travel frequently, occasionally, sometimes, or once in a blue moon, keep your toiletry bag packed and ready to go. This eliminates the time spent packing these necessities every time you travel. Remember, unless you're able to find sample-size containers for your total cleansing routine, you may have to skip a few steps while you're traveling in order to avoid bulk and weight, and purchase the necessary products once you arrive.

- If you are an exercise buff, you may need to carry another bag, but it should be just large enough to carry your exercise shoes and clothing. Before your trip, check out the exercise facilities available at your destination and bring suitable attire. This eliminates the extras for crosstrainers.

Travel Tips for Men

Following is a sample packing list for businessmen on a foray into the wide world.

- Two suits, or one suit and a navy blazer and khaki or gray trousers. For your suits, consider either gray or navy tones in solids or stripes. These colors and patterns are appropriate for any region of the country and overseas.

- Two or three shirts. Consider the weather and the length of your trip. One shirt per day will usually suffice, but two may be needed if you are traveling to very warm or humid climates.

- Packable pajamas, robe, and slippers. Consider pajamas in a lightweight cotton broadcloth, and a nylon robe. These items do not take up much room. Leave the terry robe at home.

- Interchangeable accessories. A cordovan (burgundy) colored leather belt coordinates well with most suit colors. Shoes should be kept to one pair of lace-ups and a pair of loafers. Neckties (preferably two or three) should be interchangeable and should coordinate with suits and shirts. Mixing different shirt and tie combinations with your suits and blazers will add miles to your travel wardrobe.

- Necessities like underwear, socks, and handkerchiefs should be taken in numbers appropriate to the length of your business trip.

Travel Tips for Women

For women a travel wardrobe offers several alternatives. Consider building yours around a basic color group. Navy, black, cream, camel, khaki, and gray are neutrals that could be the foundation of your travel wardrobe. To add pizzazz, include brightly colored prints and patterned blouses and shirts.

- One alternative already alluded to is the suit and dress ensemble, where the jacket coordinates with the dress for business and can be removed for evening. Another idea is a two-piece dress and a suit that complement each other. Better yet, consider two interchangeable suits, such as a black suit and a red suit, or a navy suit and a winter-white suit, or a black suit and a black-and-white houndstooth-patterned suit. Versatility is the key to these components, which add miles to any trip with minimum weight and bulk.

- Load up on accessories like scarves, jewelry, belts, and hosiery. Accessories extend the versatility of your wardrobe and help create a new look with the same pieces for each day of your trip. A black chemise dress is great with a belt and/or a scarf around the neck or dramatic jewelry for evening. Take the same black chemise and add a brightly colored jacket; if you want, belt the jacket for another new look. Put your emphasis on accessories, because they take up less space in your garment bag.

- Blouses and shirts should coordinate with suits and also be able to mix and match for distinctly different looks. Consider taking a white silk blouse, or classic print or stripe, round-neck or tailored notched collared styles for a look that means business with any suit style. Fine knit tops in polo or crew styles might also be considered, but avoid boatneck and similar styles; they have limited versatility.

- Shoes should be kept to two basic pairs, preferably pump styles with one-and-a-half to two-inch heels. For comfort, bring shoes that have been worn several times before. If you will be doing a lot of walking consider shoes with flexible soles and cushion insoles. Finally, consider basic colors like navy, black, or taupe to coordinate with your wardrobe.
- Necessities should be packed in a toiletry bag. Limit cosmetics to colors that can be worn with everything from day to evening wear and packed in a small cosmetics case. Consider taupe, teal, navy, brown, or deep purple. For other makeup essentials, consider one color of foundation, mascara, lipstick, and blush.
- Include a packable robe, nightgown, and slippers in nylon, polyester, or silk. These fabrics are lightweight and do not take up a lot of room. Keep the flannels at home.

EXERCISE

Your Travel Wardrobe

Devise your own travel wardrobe using the following chart. Consider several wardrobes to meet all your travel needs.

Clothing Item	Coordinates With	Day or Evening	Total Outfit Description
_____	_____	_____	_____
_____	_____	_____	_____
_____	_____	_____	_____
_____	_____	_____	_____
_____	_____	_____	_____
_____	_____	_____	_____
_____	_____	_____	_____
_____	_____	_____	_____

EXERCISE

Packing Tips*

Victoria A. Seitz, Ph.D.

1. Never bring more than you can carry yourself.
2. Make sure that the last items you pack are the first things you'll need when you arrive at your destination.
3. One or two color combinations that you can mix or match are the best.
4. Make a checklist.
5. Place heavier items on the bottom and things you'll need right away, like pajamas and toothbrush, on top.
6. Pack a collapsible lightweight bag if you plan to bring home more than you take.
7. A full but not overstuffed suitcase helps to keep clothes wrinkle-free.
8. Any unfilled spaces should be stuffed with tissue paper so that the contents will not slide.
9. Luggage tags should be placed on the inside of your suitcase as well as outside. For the outside tag, your business address should be used to avoid a robbery at your home while you're away.
10. A copy of your itinerary taped to the inside of your suitcase will enable airlines to locate you in the event of misrouted luggage.
11. Select clothes that are washable and drip-dry.
12. Keep two packing lists—one for short trips and one for long stays—inside your luggage.
13. Take the packing list with you so you know what you have.
14. When packing items that can wrinkle, close all buttons, zippers, and snaps.
    - Fold each item along its natural creases.
    - Drape each garment across the suitcase so that the ends hang over the sides.

- Alternate putting the top of each garment on the right and left sides so that the thickness remains uniform.
- Next fold each item around the other, alternating the over hang from right and left sides. Your garments cushion each other, thus preventing wrinkles.

15. Include a few plastic bags for dirty or damp clothes.
16. Bring sentimental items to put on the night table next to the bed.
17. When packing a hard-sided suitcase begin by putting all the heavy items like shoes and toiletry kits on the bottom near the hinges.
    - Then roll the clothes that won't wrinkle (i.e., sweaters, socks, T-shirts, and so forth) and place them around heavier items. This prevents heavy items from sliding and wrinkling clothes when carrying the suitcase.
    - Even distribution of weight also makes the case easier to carry.
18. Always have an additional small pouch packed with commonly needed items such as aspirin, bandages, or a small sewing kit.
19. Shoes should be placed in plastic bags to prevent them from soiling other clothes.
20. Small, soft items such as socks and stockings may be used to stuff clothes that easily lose shape, like a man's shirt collar.

* Preview Media, Inc. copyright 1996

THIRTEEN

Shopping Smart

Shopping Tips

Shopping is an art. Like any art, it needs practice. Part of projecting that executive image is making satisfying, quality purchases. Becoming a smart shopper takes time and the development of skills—skills to add the right purchases to your wardrobe instead of wasteful catastrophes. Here are some tips you can use on your next shopping venture that will help clear the jungle in the fashion retail world.

Set goals and objectives prior to shopping. Being specific is the key. Having completed your wardrobe inventory, you will be better able to jot down exactly what you need to get. This is just like creating a grocery shopping list. Consider writing down not only what item or items you need but also the dollar limit you would be willing to spend. This will reduce the chance of impulse shopping or of buying the first item that comes close to what you want—but is priced higher than what you would normally spend.

Pick a time when you won't be rushed, when sales people will be available to serve you. Weekends and weekday lunch hours are overwhelmed by shoppers. Moreover, give yourself enough time to shop. Haste really does make waste. You'll probably regret a hasty decision, so take your time.

■ Become aware of current fashion trends. Familiarize yourself with specific style names, such as paisley, double-breasted, fitted shirts, slim skirts, sarongs, and bolero jackets. The salesperson will be able to show you exactly what you're looking for if you know how to communicate it. Identify one or two pieces that will update your wardrobe, such as a jacket, shirt, or tie pattern for the forthcoming season, and make that addition in your shopping list.

■ Dress for your shopping venture. If you plan to purchase evening attire, remember to wear or bring along the appropriate undergarments and shoes. If you plan to purchase pants or a suit, bring the shoes and shirt you will be wearing with it. Dress comfortably. Wear flats or shoes with flexible soles that will be comfortable over a long period of time.

■ If you are trying to match or coordinate an item of clothing from your wardrobe, cut a swatch from the seam allowance of the garment and bring it with you. This will help you and the salesperson locate the right-colored item.

■ Shop alone. This may seem like a difficult task, but it's the wise thing to do. When you shop with a friend, not only do you have the friend selling to you but the salesperson too. You may end up purchasing something you had no intention of buying. Yes, it's fun to shop with someone, but if you do, don't buy. Put the item on hold if you want to, have a good time, but save that final decision for when you are alone.

Sometimes marriage partners have an arrangement where nothing is purchased without the other's say-so. In this case, you might pick out the item you wish to purchase, put it on hold, and bring your partner back to okay the purchase at another time.

Men, consider doing your wardrobe shopping yourself. Don't give this responsibility to your spouse, girlfriend, or secretary. Know your measurements. If you feel you need help, make an appointment with a personal shopper, available in many department stores, or with a personal fashion consultant, who can be located through the telephone directory.

■ Be sure to try on all items before purchasing, since sizes in the apparel industry are not standardized. Moreover, a lot of variation can be found within a single brand or size. Higher-priced clothing tends to be generous in size.

- Examine the item carefully for quality. Check for fabric flaws, stains, poor workmanship, unraveling hems and seam allowances, and missing buttons.

- Go outside the dressing room for a more accurate look in the mirror. The lighting in the dressing room often promotes an inaccurate evaluation of the clothing item with your skin color.

- Buy your shoes in the afternoon. Feet have a tendency to swell as the day progresses.

- Don't neglect the accessories. Consider the importance of the right tie, cuff link, or collar pin when purchasing your suit.

- Know the return policies of stores where purchases are made, particularly sale items. Most stores have liberal policies when it comes to regular-priced merchandise, but there may be some limitations for sale merchandise. Ask the salesperson how many days you have to return an item and whether you'll get your money back or receive a merchandise credit.

- Be sure to check fiber content and garment care information before purchasing clothing. This will save a lot of misfortune if you are someone who won't have anything dry-cleaned or who has a limited budget for it.

- Try off-price, discount, second-hand, and factory outlets, as well as catalogues, for bargains and convenience. Off-priced stores like Marshall's and Loehman's often purchase consolidated sale merchandise from department and specialty stores and pass the savings on to consumers. These stores also carry manufacturers' overruns, which are quality goods and great buys for consumers. Manufacturers' overruns are apparel items that were over-produced and undersold. Manufacturers sell these items to discount stores or in their own factory outlet stores.

    Catalogues offer substantial product information and are convenient for purchasing and returning merchandise. Spiegel, for example, will have your returned merchandise picked up at no cost to you. Other catalogue firms will cover the cost of postage on all returned purchases.

    Today, catalogue businesses are growing to meet demand for convenient shopping resources. Catalogue shopping has become a way of life for many consumers who have found that catalogue services are often superior to those offered by retail stores. Catalogues can offer better information than most retail store sales personnel, including fiber content and garment care, along with a photograph of each item. A final benefit is that orders are placed easily by phone, practically any time of day or night, through toll-free numbers and credit cards. Do make sure you choose catalogue companies with reputations for quality, companies like Spiegel, Land's End, and L. L. Bean. And look for the emblem that indicates membership in the National Direct Marketing Association. These factors will help ensure that you have a satisfactory experience.

■ Be aware of the different levels of quality and price available to today's customer, discussed at length in a later chapter. The costliest garments generally offer the most superior workmanship, as well as high-fashion styling and the best all-natural materials. However, this is not a hard-and-fast rule. In some cases you may be paying hundreds of dollars more for the designer name alone—so don't be fooled.

EXERCISE

What Is Your Shopping Style?

Using a separate sheet of paper, describe your shopping style. Note which shopping habits are good and which not so good. Then write out a step-by-step plan to enhance your shopping style.

FOURTEEN

Fitting Your Executive Image

Fit is vital to projecting an executive image. If something doesn't fit correctly, it calls attention to itself. Pants that are too tight in the hips or waist, for example, serve only to point out and emphasize your figure liabilities. To understand fit, you must get over the hurdle of size. As we have seen there is no standardized sizing. In menswear, a 34 waist in a suit pant is more generous than a 34 waist in sportswear. In womenswear, a size 8 in one brand may be equal to a size 10 in another or a size 4 in still another. For this reason it's best to concentrate on fit rather than size. In fact, you should probably ignore size altogether!

Be especially cautious of psychological sizing by manufacturers. Higher priced apparel is often deliberately cut more generously. As noted earlier, if you normally wear a size 12 dress, you will be more likely to splurge on a $500 dress if you suddenly fit a size 6. Again, think fit rather than size.

A final factor to consider when determining fit is human error. Perhaps you are familiar with a certain brand and know what size you wear in that brand. One day you try on that size 10 and it doesn't fit. Try another size 10. It could have been a mistake in manufacturing.

Basic Tips

- No gaps up front. For men and women, gaps in the front of a blouse or shirt are a distraction. They mean that the garment is too small in the chest or bust area.

  Athletically minded men may lift weights to increase your chest measurement. That's fine, if you consider what it may mean to the fit of your shirts! The result is often a large chest and neck measurement and a small waist. Consider purchasing fitted or tapered shirt styles to accommodate your physique. If you have a large chest measurement in relation to your neck and waist, consider having your shirts tailor-made. Custom shirts are not all that expensive, and your shirts will fit comfortably everywhere. This goes double for men who increase not only their chest and neck size but also their arms. A shirt with tight sleeves, whether short or long, is not macho, but simply a signal that your shirt doesn't fit.

  For women, a large bust measurement often doesn't mean a large neck, arm, or waist size. Your neck and arms are in proportion to the rest of your body measurements except the bust. There are two things you can do to overcome this problem. One is to purchase a blouse or shirt that fits comfortably over the bust area without gaps, and have the blouse altered around the neck, arms or waist. The other is to have your blouses custom made. Again, it is not as expensive as you may think, and you can curtail costs by purchasing your own fabric and notions and having a professional sew the blouse according to your measurements. (You might want to try doing it yourself.) In any case, make sure that your blouses and shirts lie smoothly over the front and that sweaters are not tight in the bust. Remember, ill-fitting apparel draws attention to figure flaws.

- Pants and skirts should fit smoothly over the legs and derriere. This is probably one of the worst areas for poor fit. Ample ease of one to two inches should be given in the waist, hip, and thigh area.

  For men, some indications of pants not fitting properly are too much fabric in the seat of the pants, the stomach extending over the front waistline of the pant, the pants riding on the hips rather than on the waist or being tight in the thigh, flesh extending out and over the pant waist at the sides and back, and tightness in the rear. Pants should fit comfortably around the waist with no overhang around the middle. If there is too much fabric in the seat of the pants, have the excess removed. Pants should ride over the hip and thigh area with enough ease to allow freedom of movement. The side seam of the pant should be straight down the side. Pockets should not spread apart to show the pocket lining. Pants should fit smoothly over the buttocks with enough ease to allow freedom of movement.

Some brands of pants for men are created to give more ease in the hips and thighs. "Levis for Men" are an example. Like women, men tend to get larger from the waist down as they get older.

For women, the rules for pants are about the same, but with a few more considerations. Pants should have ample ease in the waist, hip, thigh, and crotch. If your hips are large but you have a small waist, go up a size and have the waist altered. If you have a flat derriere, have the back seam of the pants taken in to eliminate excess fabric. Be sure the pants lie smoothly over the hip and thigh area, minimizing curves. If the fabric is stretched around the thighs or hips, the pants are too small. Be sure the pants fit securely around the waist with sufficient ease. The crotch area should be long enough to fit comfortably. Too short a crotch will not only be uncomfortable but will affect the fit in the back.

With skirts, proper fit is just as important for comfort and for camouflaging figure flaws as with pants. If a skirt starts riding up on the hips, it's too tight. If it's showing stretch lines across the hips and thighs, it's too tight. When excess fabric appears near the waist in back, either the skirt is too tight in the hips or you have a sway back. In the latter case you might consider having excess fabric removed from the back waist in the form of deep darts. On the other hand, if your hips are large and your waist small, go up a size or two and have the waist taken in.

■ Shoulder seams should rest close to the shoulder bone. Given the number of off-the-shoulder styles, it is easy to become confused as to the proper fit of jackets and shirts. Locate your shoulder bone and use it as a guide. This will allow ample ease in the underarm and back areas of jackets and shirts without their appearing too large.

With attention to fit, we are talking about set-in sleeves, the kinds of sleeves found on most dress shirts, blouses, suit jackets, and sports jackets. The underarm area of a set-in sleeve is crucial to comfort. If the shoulder seam falls short of the shoulder bone, the underarm area will be too tight and very uncomfortable, and the back will appear stretched. If the shoulder seam falls too far past the bone, the garment will appear too large. Comfort is the key, but if you are unsure, enlist the keen eye of a tailor or seamstress to help determine the proper shoulder fit.

- Collars and cuffs should not pinch. When the shirt is buttoned to the top, you should be able to slide two fingers in and out of the collar; one to two in and out of the cuffs.

- Shoes should fit comfortably the first time. Remember when you were small and the salesman would measure your feet and press his index finger to make sure you had enough room at the front of the shoe? Those steps are just as important today. Don't be fooled by the line that the shoes will become more comfortable as they are worn, or that once you break them in they will be enjoyable to wear all day long. Shoes should fit comfortably the first time, every time. If your shoes don't fit, your attitude won't be very fitting either!

Make sure to shop for shoes in the afternoon, because feet swell as the day progresses. To check the shoe size, stand with your feet spread apart, equal weight placed on each foot. There should be an index-finger's space between your longest toe and the end of the shoe. Make sure the widest part of your foot lines up with the widest part of the shoe.

Try shoes on with the proper hosiery. If you are trying on running shoes, wear athletic socks. If you are trying on pumps, bring along knee-highs. Even if you don't plan on wearing hosiery with the shoe, a nylon knee-high or thin sock will aid in determining proper fit.

Check the inside of the shoe for seams or other sources of potential discomfort by running your finger along the inside of the shoe. Walk, jog, or bounce in them to determine comfort. Walk, if you can, on both carpeted and hard surfaces, since these surfaces affect shoe comfort differently. When walking, the heel of the shoe should fit snugly on the heel; the front of the shoe should not pinch the top of the foot.

- Ties should fit securely around the neck and end at the middle of the belt buckle. It is important that when the tie is tied, the knot not be loose or appear to be floating. If you happen to be long-waisted or simply tall, you'll need a long tie, available most commonly at tall men's shops.

- The jacket should fit comfortably. Whether you are a man or woman, your jacket should lie smoothly at the neck and cover the curvature of the buttocks. The sleeves should land at the wrist bone or slightly below. Shirts should extend a half-inch beyond the end of the jacket sleeve.

    When you are sitting, the buttoned jacket should fit loosely. There should be no tugging between the arms in the back of the jacket, and there should be ample ease in the armholes. When you are standing, the buttoned jacket should fit smoothly over the front of the wearer. It should also button at the waist or slightly below, not above. Lapels should roll smoothly, without wrinkles. Breast and waist pockets of the jacket should lie smoothly too. Back vents of the jacket should be properly aligned and not apart.

- Proper length is essential. Pants should be hemmed when you are wearing the shoes you intend to wear with the pants. They should fall straight, with a slight break at the top of the shoe. At the back of the pant, the hem should land at the point or slightly above where the sole and the leather upper meet. This means pants that are slightly longer in the back (about three-quarters of an inch) than in the front. Pant hems should not touch the ground; this will destroy the fabric. Cuffs are optional for men in business, but the same criteria apply when determining the length for cuffed pants. Cuffs should hang horizontally and be about one and one-half inch in width. Cuffs not only create a new look, but add extra weight to the pant hem as well.

    Regarding lengths of skirts for women, extremes should be avoided. The most attractive skirt length for women is right around the knee. The length you desire can vary, however, up to a point. If you desire a shorter length, be certain that it's comfortable to function in. One to two inches above the knee is about tops. Remember, it should not only feel comfortable to you but also complement your figure.

As noted earlier, if you desire a longer length, you should avoid anything past the midcalf. At that point, the look becomes not only dowdy but hazardous. If you have wide calves, the best length is right at your knee. When you wear your hems at the widest point of the calf, the horizontal line of the hem makes them appear even wider.

EXERCISE

Proper Fit

To help you determine what is the best fit for you, spend the day trying on different brands in different stores. Be sure to try on different garment pieces in various sizes and note their fit on you. Record the best fit for future reference by noting the brands and sizes and why they are the right fit for you.

FIFTEEN

Spotting Quality

Whether it costs $15, $250, or $1,000, high-quality apparel is the key to projecting the executive image. Why? It tells others that you appreciate the good things in life, particularly the people who work with or for you. In today's economy, furthermore, where every dollar counts, clothing purchases must be made to last their worth.

Quality is related to how garments are costed by manufacturers. Manufacturers strive to maintain quality in styling and construction within price levels. Six primary price levels are used to identify apparel goods: couture, designer, bridge, better, moderate, and budget.

To some, "couture" describes astronomically priced items in a ready-to-wear designer collection. However, true haute couture is made-to-order apparel. Haute couture is the ultimate in quality, fit, and style. Clothing is constructed using the finest workmanship and luxurious fabrics of high thread counts. Couture apparel offers the potential for future alterations by providing generous seam allowances. For some people, couture apparel is the best clothing investment. But it is definitely not for everyone. The prices of these apparel items are extremely high. A Chanel suit may run close to $14,000 and a matching blouse $3,000.

Clothing items marketed as "designer" items are seen as fashion forward and should be of extremely high quality, though this is not always the case. Clothing at this price level is styled from high-quality fabrics without custom fit. Designers have a preference for working with luxurious fabrics like cashmere and silk; unfortunately, wholesale costs of these fabrics increase yearly, resulting in higher price tags for consumers. "Designer" apparel includes Geoffrey Beene, Perry Ellis, Christian Dior, Pierre Cardin, and Yves Saint-Laurent, to name several.

"Bridge" apparel is the newest and fastest-growing category in men's and women's apparel. It represents a price and style range that falls between "designer" and so-called "better" merchandise. Examples of "bridge" apparel include Anne Klein II, Calvin Klein Classics, Perry Ellis Portfolio, and Ralph Lauren Classics. These labels are spinoffs from designer collections and offer classic styling made with less expensive fabrics at more affordable prices. "Bridge" apparel also offers consumers consistent fit.

"Better" merchandise includes seasonless, classically-styled apparel priced lower than "designer" and "bridge" merchandise. They are manufactured from less expensive fabrics purchased in bulk; quality of construction and fit are satisfactory. "Better" merchandise offers a lot of fashion for the money—an entire outfit may cost between $300 and $500. "Better" merchandise lines include Liz Claiborne, J.G. Hook, Lloyd Williams, Evan Picone, J.H. Collectibles, Jones New York, John Henry, Lacoste, and Gunne Sax.

"Moderate" apparel includes the clothing most Americans buy for everyday wear. Consumers can put together an outfit for about $150 to $300. Moderate lines include Marona, Gloria Vanderbilt, Koret, Russ, Haggar, Arrow, Buster Brown, and Healthtex. Again, less-expensive fabrics and limited hand workmanship result in high-volume merchandise at moderate prices. Durability is also limited, possibly resulting in higher maintenance costs than "better," "bridge," or "designer" merchandise. For example, seam finishes may be missing or inadequate, and allowances may prove less than ample. Closures may not be secure and additional buttons may not be included. But consumers should not dismiss this category for clothing investments. With a keen eye for quality, consumers can determine their value for the price.

"Budget" merchandise is created from lower-quality fabrics. Manufacturers reduce production costs by selecting time-saving construction techniques, often resulting in garments that do not fit well and that fail to present a pleasing appearance. Garments are constructed with inferior thread and fasteners, and styling may be limited. However, someone with an eye trained in spotting high quality will be able to recognize long-term benefits in some of these apparel items.

What a particular retailer, as opposed to manufacturer, defines as "haute couture," "designer," "bridge," "better," "moderate," and "budget" varies a great deal. Liz Claiborne may be considered "designer" merchandise in one store because it's the highest priced merchandise there, but be found in the "better" area in another store where Ralph Lauren and Calvin Klein are the highest priced. For this reason it's important for consumers to be able to recognize high-quality apparel *before they enter the store*. Although different kinds of stores may vary in how they label their merchandise, most carry only one or two price levels.

Specialty stores offer up-to-date fashions, high in quality and selection. Such stores focus on one particular or related product category and so can offer "designer," "bridge," "better," or "moderate" merchandise. Specialty stores reflect a high degree of fashion awareness pertaining to their particular category. In addition, they provide more personalized services that may be helpful in the selection of a wardrobe. Such specialty stores include Casual Corner, The Limited, Lerners, Victoria's Secret, Chess King, FootAction, USA, The Gap, and, on a larger scale, Saks Fifth Avenue.

Department stores offer limited assortments in heavy quantities. However, such stores cater to the mainstream of shoppers and offer high-quality "bridge," "better," and "moderate" merchandise. Each store or chain reflects a particular image, demonstrated in the level of quality and price appropriate for the target consumer. Remember, though, no matter the store or name on the label, *you* must check for quality. Even designer merchandise can be faulty, as experience will testify. Because most manufacturers represent several designers, department stores, and so on, it's apparent that what most people are paying for with designer and bridge merchandise is the name. I believe that you can find quality at any price if you familiarize yourself with quality cues.

Introducing quality control in your clothing purchases will certainly aid in satisfactory purchases down the road. Here are some further cues for spotting quality in your next purchase.

- Check for proper labeling securely attached to the garment. Each garment, as directed by law, should have a label(s) with fiber content, country of origin, care instructions, and manufacturer's name. Fiber percentages must be given on the label in descending order, with those representing less than 5 percent of the fabric identified as "miscellaneous."

  If the garment is trimmed in another fabric, ask yourself these questions: Will the trim wash the same as the rest of the garment? If not, is it detachable? Will the color of trim fade or run on the rest of the garment?

- If you are buying a plaid or striped garment, does the pattern match at the seams? This is the sign of a well-made garment. It takes more fabric to match the plaids and stripes but creates a much more pleasing overall appearance. Check the side, back, shoulder, leg, and sleeve seams to make sure they match. If purchasing a plaid or striped jacket, button it and check to make sure the pattern matches in front.

- The interfacing should lie smoothly. Interfacings are used to provide extra body and support to collars, cuffs, waistbands, shirt front plackets, and jacket lapels. To keep the cost of apparel down, many manufacturers are now using a synthetic interfacing called "pelon," which is heat-set on the fabric. Sometimes the heat is not applied properly, and the interfacing pulls away from the fabric. This can create bubbles in the fabric, so be on the lookout. Check also to make sure that the interfacing is of an appropriate stiffness for the fabric. For example, putting a very stiff interfacing with a soft rayon fabric will ruin the drape of the fabric.

- Check for flaws and stains. Some manufacturers, concerned with producing high-quality garments, have invested in a large frame that allows for examination of the fabric before it is used. However, this is not the case with all. Be vigilant. Check for quality.

  If the garment has a stain, such as rust, pass it by; you cannot remove rust stains. With some fabrics, such as raw silk, flaws are part of their beauty. This information should be noted on the manufacturer's tag. If the fabric has a flaw and this is not mentioned on the tag, pass it up. If the garment is a knit, check to make sure the fabric contains no runs.

- Check to make sure that the top and bottom of the outfit are the same color. This is particularly important for suits and two or three-piece outfits. When the fabric is dyed, a certain yardage of it is placed in a large dye bath, then put on bolts. This process is repeated until the specified amount of dyed fabric is completed. Sometimes, however, the same fabric will not absorb the dye in the same manner as before, resulting in fabrics that differ slightly in color. It frequently happens in the manufacturing process that the fabric is not inspected for this problem, resulting in coordinated outfits and suits with different shades of color in the top and bottom. This can happen to any manufacturer, so even when the label spells quality, make sure to compare both items for color equality.

  If the color looks different in the store, it will be different at home. Check the garment in different lighting. For example, if you are in the interior of the store under fluorescent lighting, ask to examine the garment under natural light near a window in the store, and vice versa. If the color does differ, point this out to the salesperson. He or she may wish to break the suit or outfit apart and sell it as separates.

- Check seam allowances to make sure the seams are finished. If the garment is not lined, body movements put wear and tear on the interior of the garment and unfinished seams will unravel. This will begin as soon as the garment is washed. So examine the seam allowance for some kind of finish, an over stitch, a zigzag stitch, pinking, turning under, or stitching. This should be apparent on knitted as well as woven garments.

- Check the seams for puckering. When garments are sewn in factories, many fabrics are run through the same sewing machine without any adjustment to tension. When the tension is too tight for a particular fabric, seams can pucker. Don't think you can iron this flaw out. A little puckering will always be apparent and will affect the hang of the garment. The seams should be pressed flat and open to avoid bulges.

- Check the buttons for secure attachment and appearance. To curtail costs, many manufacturers cut down on thread. Check each button to make sure thread is running through every attaching hole. Tug on them slightly to see whether they are loose. If you don't mind replacing loose buttons, purchase the garment anyway. However, don't expect it to last a lifetime. Check to see whether extra buttons come with the garment. If not, check with the salesperson; the department may have a drawerfull. While you're at it, check every button to make sure it is not cracked, chipped, or broken.

- Check the pockets for quality. Inseam pockets are often a combination of the principal fabric and the lining, usually in cotton, acetate, or nylon. If you can see the lining when you try on the garment, don't buy it. Apparently the fashion fabric did not go far enough into the pocket. Make sure, too, that the lining fabric complements the fashion fabric and does not show through. For example, a thick lining fabric will add extra bulk, which will be apparent. A navy lining with a winter-white skirt will also be hard to ignore.

- When purchasing a lined jacket, pant, or skirt, check the quality of the lining construction. Does the lining show at the hemline? Skirt and pant linings should be attached at the waistline and hemmed separately from the garment.

- When purchasing a gathered garment, look for a consistent flow of gathers; or if the garment is pleated, be sure the pleats are evenly spaced and alike in pleat width and depth.

- When buying a suit, check to make sure that the lapels roll softly and lie flat against the chest. The lining should fit loosely in the jacket for comfort. Make sure there is a rear pleat along the back seam of the jacket lining.

- Check buttonholes for quality. They should be even, with closely spaced stitches and no loose threads.

- Check the inside of the garment as well as the outside. Don't be fooled by a perfect exterior; if what is on the inside is inadequate, it will limit the life of your investment. Check that seam allowances are finished, that buttons are attached securely, and that buttonholes show no loose threads. Check to make sure that patterns match at seams and garment closings, that no fabric flaws or stains are apparent and that tops and bottoms match in color. Check all aspects of the garment and you'll be happier for it.

EXERCISE

Go shopping. Go to a department store and take note of the brands and designer labels in each area or department. Go to a specialty store and do the same thing. In both stores, inspect items for quality. Is there a difference? What is the predominant fiber content at each location—natural or synthetic? What are the prevalent styles—fashion forward, classic, or conservative? This will take a whole day to do, so give yourself plenty of time to jot down your observations.

SIXTEEN

The Psychology of Color

You see a red fire truck, lights flashing, siren blaring. Automatically, your heart begins to race, your eyes dilate, and your blood pressure rises.

Did you know that red is the most physically provocative color? Why do we wear blue when we're blue? When you want to feel perky or need a pick-me-up, do you find yourself dressing in bright colors? Why do nurses and doctors wear white uniforms? Do you get the same feeling from a well-lit room filled with bright colors as from a dimly-lit room in muted colors? Is there such a thing as the "power tie"?

Color is probably the most important element of design. It influences emotions. It helps us to express ourselves as individuals. It influences our impressions of others, as well. Color is also one of the most important features drawing someone to a clothing item for closer examination in a store or catalogue.

Color reveals personality and can symbolize many things. It can be used, for example, to create positive environments in hospitals and office buildings. You can use color to solicit specific responses from others, to dramatic effect.

Certain religions use color to specify holy days and seasons, such as Lent. Color can also mark important life events, such as marriage and death. It is also used to distinguish one social group or entity from another, as in the case of school colors.

Here are some common psychological associations of colors:

- **Red:** Hot, dangerous, angry, passionate, sentimental, exciting, vibrant, and aggressive.
- **Orange:** Lively, cheerful, joyous, warm, energetic, hopeful, and hospitable.
- **Yellow:** Bright, sunny, cheerful, warm, prosperous, cowardly, and deceitful.
- **Green:** Calm, cool, fresh, friendly, pleasant, balanced, restful, lucky, envious, and immature.
- **Blue:** Peaceful, calm, restful, highly esteemed, serene, tranquil, truthful, cool, formal, spacious, sad, and depressed.
- **Purple:** Royal, dignified, powerful, rich, dominating, dramatic, mysterious, wise, and passionate.
- **White:** Innocent, youthful, faithful, pure, and peaceful.
- **Black:** Mysterious, tragic, serious, sad, dignified, silent, old, sophisticated, strong, wise, evil, and gloomy.
- **Gray:** Modest, sad, and old.

When considering what colors to wear, bear in mind that too much color can make an ensemble appear gaudy; too little can make it appear drab. Here are some further color tips to help you project your executive image.

- Black is best for formal attire. It creates a feeling of sophistication, as with the black tuxedo. Black is now becoming a popular color for men's suits.
- Brown is considered casual in some parts of the country and is usually not worn for business. In the mid- and southwest, however, brown, camel, and beige tones are worn often. Wheat, a member of the brown family, is commonly seen in sport coats throughout the United States, especially in summer. Cinnamon, which is a mixture of red and brown and which has been prevalent in women's apparel in the past several years, is also quite acceptable.
- Navy makes everyone look good, whether fair or olive-complexioned. It's great for classic styles, such as suits, as well as for blazers, skirts,

and trousers. The nautical look, commonly seen during resort and spring seasons, draws its associations from the cool feeling of navy. Navy gives the feeling of individual authority when worn in business.

- Beige and gray elicit a tailored and professional image. Gray in charcoal tones elicits a sophisticated professionalism, while camel and beige elicit a quiet, unassuming professionalism. Both colors give a feeling of group authority.

- White is best accessorized with other colors (off-white is best for most complexions). Use white for shirts and blouses and winter white in blazers, trousers, and skirts.

- Red, green, and blue in assorted tints and shades are suitable for all occasions. Pick the best shade or tint for your skin tone. Women, avoid pastel reds, blues, and greens for main clothing pieces; they give an overly feminine feeling, which can affect others' impressions of your professionalism. Green is not an acceptable suit color for men or women, but teal or forest green can be introduced in ties or plaid sport coats for men and in suits, jackets, and skirts for women.

- Yellow is most appropriate for casual clothing; however, vibrant yellows are becoming common in women's jackets and men's ties.

- Bright colors, such as fuchsia and turquoise, are appropriate accent colors to accompany neutrals for women and in ties for men.

- Dark, cool, and dull colors make forms appear smaller. "Slimming" colors include navy, black, dark blue-violet, charcoal gray, chocolate brown, burgundy, olive, and forest green.

- Light, warm, and bright colors make forms appear larger. Such colors are white, yellow, orange, and red.

- Use no more than three colors in the main pieces of a clothing ensemble.

- If you are a shy person, incorporate red in your clothing ensemble in order to be taken more assertively. Yes, this means the red "power tie" for men.

- If you are overly aggressive, wear navy, beige, camel, and gray in your main wardrobe pieces in order to be perceived as more approachable. If you are a large person, tall and big-framed, you may also want to introduce more beige, camel, grays, and navies in your wardrobe.

Selecting the Right Colors for You

I didn't realize the impact of wearing the right colors with my skin, eye, and hair color until I had my colors "done." What a difference it made in the colors I chose for myself.

Of course, although certain colors may look better with your skin tone than others, it's important to wear the ones you feel good in and for which you receive compliments. But if you want to know which colors are best for your skin tone, the information that follows should help.

Nowadays it is popular to divide skin, hair, and eye color into four categories: "Winter," "Summer," "Spring," and "Fall." To learn what category you are in, turn to page 133. Winter and Summer have blue undertones, while Spring and Fall have yellow undertones. You can also think of these two divisions as "cool" (blue) and "warm" (yellow). If you fall into the "warm" category, select warm colors, shades, or tints like red, yellow, and orange, but also warm versions of the cool colors, like teal, sky blue, and red-purple.

If you fall into the "cool" category, select cool colors, shades, or tints like blue, navy, green, and purple, as well as cool versions of the warm colors—burgundy, chocolate brown, fuchsia, and chartreuse.

Perhaps you're a combination of seasons. Perhaps your skin and eyes are winter and your hair summer. How would you approach this? Since they are both cool seasons, wear predominantly cool-based colors. If you're a combination of Spring and Autumn, the warm seasons, wear predominantly warm-based colors. If you happen to be a mixture of warm and cool colors—say you have a warm hair color with olive (cool) complexion and brown eyes (cool)—go with the predominant temperature, cool, in your wardrobe selections.

If you are planning to change your hair color, by all means check with a hairdresser first. If you are currently a winter, you might want to color your hair in a cool-based color such as brown with a burgundy cast, silver gray, blonde ash, or blue gray.

Winter:

Skin: Blue or blue-pink undertones
Very white
Beige
Brown
Rosy beige
Olive
Black (blue undertones)
Charcoal-brown freckles

Hair: Blue-black
Medium brown
Dark brown
Salt and pepper
Silver gray
White blonde
White

Eyes: Dark red-brown
Black-brown
Hazel
Gray blue
Blue with white flecks in iris
Dark blue
Gray-green
Green with white flecks in iris

Colors:

Navy	Red
Black	White
Shocking pink	Gray
Purple	Chocolate brown
Taupe	Blue
Burgundy	Forest green
Chartreuse	Blueberry

Summer:

Skin: Blue undertone
Pale beige (pink cheeks)
Pale beige
Very pink
Rosy or charcoal brown freckles
Gray-brown

Hair: Platinum blonde
Ash blonde (grayish cast)
Dark brown (taupe tone)
Brown (auburn cast)
Blue-gray
Pearl white

Eyes: Blue (brown around pupil)
Gray-blue
Gray-green
Pale gray
Blue (white flecks)
Green (white flecks)
Hazel
Bright clear blue
Clear, pale aqua
Soft brown

Colors:

Soft blues	Rose pink
Navy	Mauve
Plum	Rose-brown
Lavender	Blue-gray
Ice beige	Sea blue
Slate gray	Raspberry
Taupe	Pale green
Dusty coral	Seafoam

Spring:

Skin: Golden undertone
Ivory
Ivory with pale golden freckles
Peach
Golden beige
Rosy cheeks

Hair: Flaxen blonde
Golden blonde
Strawberry blonde
Auburn
Golden brown
Red-black
Golden gray

Eyes: Blue with white rays
Clear blue (brown flecks)
Aqua
Bright blue (turquoise)
Light golden brown
Clear green
Teal

Colors:

Golden brown	Peach
Camel	Soft blues
Peachy pink	Golden yellow
Ivory	Periwinkle
Marine blue	Coral
Bright green	Turquoise
Aqua	Soft yellow
Tangerine	Jade
Cream	

Autumn:

Skin: Golden undertone
Ivory
Ivory with freckles
Peach (sometimes with freckles)
Golden beige
Dark beige (coppery)
Golden brown

Hair: Red
Coppery red-brown
Chestnut brown
Golden brown
Charcoal black
Golden gray
Auburn

Eyes: Dark brown
Golden brown
Amber
Hazel (golden brown)
Green (brown or gold flecks)
Pale, clear green
Blue with aqua tone

Colors:

Turquoise	Teal
Orange	Brick red
Gold	Moss green
Emerald	Camel
Mustard	Gold
Dark brown	Warm beige
Sea blue	Olive
Clay	Celadon
Banana	Butterscotch
Royal blue	Ivory
Cream	Salmon

EXERCISE

Using your wardrobe inventory, list below the colors most prominent in your wardrobe. Then list those that are scarce. Star (*) those colors on which you receive compliments when you wear them. Reread this chapter and jot down what color is saying about the person you are.

The colors in my wardrobe are . . .

1. ....
2. ....
3. ....
4. ....
5. ....

6. ....
7. ....
8. ....
9. ....
10. ....

What do these colors say about me?

....
....
....
....
....

EXERCISE

SEVENTEEN

The Elements and Principles of Design

The Essence of Successful Coordination

Looking through fashion magazines or attending fashion shows, you may wonder how designers and other fashion experts put it all together. How do they create? How do they know what goes with what? How do they do it?

With their sense of style and taste, people in the fashion industry have the tools to invent and coordinate fabulous fashions from season to season. The look of an executive is projected through the same tasteful and stylish coordination. Having it all together in the clothing your wear projects the executive image you desire.

By getting to know the tools of the trade you, too, can put your executive look together with flair. These tools are referred to as the *elements and principles of design* and are the essence of successful coordination. The *elements* include line, form or shape, space, texture, and color. The *principles* of design are about method and aesthetics; they include proportion, balance, rhythm, and emphasis.

Elements

Let's talk about the elements first. *Line* is a major element in design. In fact, it is the simplest form of representation. Certain lines elicit particular feelings. For example, straight lines suggest rigidity and precision. Curved lines express femininity and gracefulness. Zigzag lines express nervousness, forcing the eye to shift abruptly. Vertical lines represent stability; horizontal lines, tranquility. Diagonal lines represent action and movement. Business suits incorporate many vertical lines in their design, suggesting stability and tradition.

Line is created in two ways. First there are structural lines, like the vertical lines of skirt pleats, the straight lines of topstitching, and the curved lines of raglan sleeves, which follow the shoulders when the sleeves and bodice are sewn together.

Decorative lines are represented in fabric patterns, buttons, epaulets, and so on. These are for aesthetic purposes and usually serve no explicit function.

Study the lines in garments when coordinating outfits. Determine the predominant line direction—straight, vertical, and so on. Perhaps you have a pleated skirt with predominantly straight vertical lines. Top it with a blazer and a tailored, notch-collar blouse. Perhaps you want to wear a pair of double-pleated, cuffed trousers. Top it with a button-down pin-point oxford shirt and a blazer. Most of the lines in this ensemble are straight and vertical as well.

Line can be used to create illusions about body proportions. If you are round in shape, you can counteract this and create the illusion of angularity by wearing tailored clothing that incorporates straight and vertical lines. If you are petite and want to appear taller, you also might incorporate more vertical lines in your wardrobe selections.

Another design element is *form*. Form describes the garment shape and shapes within the garment and can express feelings and emotions. For example, rounded shapes express femininity, while long rectangles give the feeling of stability. Unlike line, which only occupies the dimension of length, form includes width and depth. For example, form can describe a garment silhouette as full or body-conscious, tubular, or bell-shaped (the trapeze dress). It can also describe shapes within a garment, like square shapes for patch pockets, round shapes for puffed sleeves, and cylinder shapes for long sleeves.

Form can create illusions as well as elicit feelings. If you are slim and angular, you may want to incorporate round shapes to counteract this angularity. If you are overweight, you might incorporate long rectangular shapes to create a slimmer appearance.

Space is the background of the design. In a picture of the countryside, space is the field in which the horse is standing. In patterned fabrics the design or pattern is the foreground and the background is the space.

Space also comes into play in the placement of buttons, pockets, and zippers. These can be placed uniformly across the garment, in one part, all over, or sporadically throughout. For example, let's take a shift dress. This is the space we have to work with. We could divide this space in two by a seam down the middle, by having red on one side and white on the other, or by putting rows of buttons down the front.

Texture is another element of design and deals with our sense of touch. Textures can be warm or cold. Warm textures are literally warm to the touch: Light is absorbed into the fabric, causing it to appear dull rather than shiny. Warm textures include wool flannel, cotton, raw silk, fuzzy sweaters, flannel nightgowns, and corduroy. Cool textures are cool, smooth, and almost slippery to the touch. Often they reflect light creating a shiny appearance. Cool textures include silk, satin, nylon, polished cotton, lame, and taffeta. When coordinating an outfit you generally want to put warm textures together and cool textures together. A fuzzy sweater goes well with flannel trousers because of similarity in texture temperature.

Textures can also be used to create illusions. If you are very thin you can create the illusion that you are larger with warm, bulky textures and cool, shiny fabrics. Large persons will want to avoid these textures and concentrate on dull, smooth fabrics such as worsted wool, wool flannel, or cotton. If you are large on the bottom but small on top, you can create a proportioned appearance by wearing a shiny, cool or bulky, warm texture on top and a warm, thin fabric on bottom.

The final element of design is *color*. Color is the most useful of the tools, as you'll realize after learning more about it. Color, too, influences moods and emotions. For example, a black dress elicits a formal, sophisticated feel; white, innocence. But there's a lot more to color than that. To understand the dynamics of this element let's acquaint you with the common terminology surrounding color.

- A *hue* is another name for color.
- A *tint* is a color with white added to it, such as pink.
- A *shade* is a color with black added to it, such as burgundy.

- *Value* is the lightness or darkness of a color.
- A *tone* is a color with gray added to it, such as gray-blue or cadet blue.
- *Intensity* is the purity of a color. When a color is intense or bright, the hue is in its purest form. To dull or lower the intensity of a hue, add its complement. For example, the color red, alone, is intense. As we add its complement, green, in varying amounts, we dull the color and the red loses its intensity.
- Colors from the same color family, like light blue and dark blue, are called *monochromatic colors*.
- Colors that are opposite one another on the color wheel are referred to as *complementary colors*. The complement of red is green; the complement of yellow is purple; the complement of orange is blue.
- Colors that are next to one another on the color wheel are called *analogous colors*. Orange is analogous to red, blue to green, yellow to orange, and purple to blue. Analogous colors coordinate well together, as do those with contrasting values.

You can use color to create illusions. If you're large-busted, for example, avoid bright colors in tops in favor of dull, grayed colors, reserving the lighter colors for skirts and pants. If petite, wear clothing items from the same color family so that the eye flows from top to bottom. For example, you might combine a navy suit with a teal blouse. Ultra-sheer charcoal gray hose would have a further lengthening effect with this ensemble. Here is why. Color is a form of light, and each color has its own wavelength. Red and yellow have longer wavelengths than blue or purple. When we look at someone who is wearing a red blouse with a navy skirt, our eyes have to stop for a moment to adjust to the differences in wavelengths. This doesn't take long, perhaps a split second, but that's enough. The result is that the person looks shorter, cut in half so to speak. That's why it's better, if you are petite, to focus on monochromatic color schemes. The eye flows from top to bottom without having to stop and adjust.

Reds, yellows, and oranges are warm colors; they appear to advance and make areas larger. Using these colors in shirts and blouses can make a small top appear larger. Warm colors can also be used to direct attention to certain body parts. For example, a navy dress with a yellow yoke draws the eye upward to the face. A yellow or red tie has the same effect.

Blues, greens, and violets suggest coolness and rest. Garments in these colors appear to recede, making the area they cover appear smaller. If you have large hips, wearing greens, blues, and violets in skirts or pants will make them appear smaller and less noticeable.

Principles

Now on to the *principles* of design, the how-tos of coordination. Given the tools of design, how do you incorporate them in a pleasing manner? The principles, again, are *balance, proportion, emphasis, rhythm, unity,* and *harmony.*

Balance suggests that if an imaginary line is drawn down the middle of an outfit, each side has equal weight. Imagine two people of the same weight on a seesaw. They are balanced. The same holds true for apparel. There are two kinds of balance: *formal* and *informal*. Formal, or symmetrical, balance is when each side of the imaginary line is the same. A shirt with pockets on each side and a double-breasted jacket with the same formation of buttons on each side are formally balanced. Formal balance creates a feeling of stability and confidence.

The other kind of balance is called informal, or asymmetrical, balance. Informal balance suggests that although each side of the imaginary line is different, the feeling of the same weight on each side is achieved. A large blue patch pocket and a small bright yellow pocket on the other is an example of informal balance. Asymmetrical balance is considered more interesting to the eye and more dramatic than symmetrical balance.

The next principal is *proportion*. Imagine you are an architect putting together a building model: every part of that model must be to scale, in proportion to every other part and to the whole building. Well, the same applies to apparel. Each part of each garment should be in proportion to the other parts and to the whole outfit. Each part, furthermore, should be in proportion to the wearer. The various parts of a shirt, such as the collar, cuffs, and buttons, should be in proportion to each other as well as to the whole outfit and to the wearer. Small fabric prints, tiny buttons, and small details are out of proportion on a large person. A shirt with a large collar and buttons is out of proportion with pants that have tiny details. In this case, you should wear pants with large details, like a large print, or that have no details at all.

With proportion we are also talking about the *ratio* of the top to the bottom. If we divide an outfit into parts, a pleasing ratio would be 2:3, rather than 1:2. A 2:3 ratio might be a long jacket with a short skirt, a short jacket with pants, an oversized long jacket with city shorts, or a blazer and pants. In a 2:3 ratio you divide the outfit into three equal parts. In the long jacket, short skirt example, the jacket is two parts to the skirt's one. In the short jacket and pants example, the jacket is one part and the pants are two. In a 1:2 ratio the top and bottom are equal, as with a long jacket and an equally long skirt. This ratio is not as pleasing to the eye as a 2:3 ratio.

The next principle is *emphasis*. Emphasis suggests a dominant point of interest. Emphasis should lead the eye to your best asset—your face. Wearing a neck scarf, earrings, and chains draws the eye upward toward the face. So does the tie. When coordinating outfits and accessorizing, you'll want to achieve one point or area of emphasis. It may be an interesting belt, tie, or scarf; however, it's important to remember that there should be one point of emphasis, not two. Emphasis can be achieved through contrast in size, color, texture, line, or shape of an apparel item or accessory. To find out what the point of emphasis is, take a quick look in the mirror. What catches your eye first is the point of emphasis.

Rhythm in dress is like rhythm in music. It's that constant, repetitive beat that keeps the music going at the same tempo. In dress, rhythm can be the repetition of color, texture, shape, or line that creates a unified feeling. It can be the progression or gradual increase or decrease of similar shapes, lines, colors, or textures in an ensemble. It can also be achieved through a radial arrangement, where lines emerge from a central point like rays. Rhythm is most commonly exercised in the first two methods.

When coordinating outfits, repeating the color, line, texture, or shape pulls the ensemble together. Combine a tailored skirt that has a lot of straight lines with a blouse that also has a lot of straight lines, like a pleated front style. When accessorizing, try a scarf that has angular shapes as the dominant pattern. If your suit has a muted pattern in several colors, repeat some of the colors in the shirt or tie or in a silk scarf in the breast pocket. The colors don't have to match exactly, nowadays, so experiment.

An example of coordinating an outfit through progression might include putting together a light blue top, a darker cummerbund, and a navy skirt or pant. Progression in shape might be ruffles that start out small in the bodice and gradually increase in the direction of the pants or skirt.

The last two principals of design are *unity* and *harmony*. When all the pieces are pulled together in an outfit, there should be a unified look. If something is missing, like a scarf, belt, or jacket, then the ensemble is not unified. How do you know when an outfit is unified? You look in the mirror and feel that everything is together. It's when you feel that something's missing that the outfit is not unified. Pieces that complete the look are missing. For example, when you wear a skirt and a blouse alone, the outfit is not unified. Pull it together with a belt, jewelry, hosiery, perhaps a scarf and/or cardigan. For men, the suit, shirt, and tie may have colors in common, but the outfit really comes together with a belt, shoes, socks, and pocket square.

Hand in hand with unity is harmony. Like harmony in music, harmony in clothing suggests commonality in color, line, shape, and texture. However, too much harmony creates monotony. An outfit that has too much harmony might be a blue tailored top and a dark blue tailored bottom. To introduce variation for interest's sake, tie a floral patterned scarf around your neck, campfire style. The floral pattern introduces not only other colors but also rounded shapes. Now the look appears harmonious, not monotonous. Another example might be the standard suit, shirt, and tie. All of these pieces have an abundance of straight, vertical lines. Introduce a floral or paisley pattern tie and the monotony is broken.

Using the elements and principles of design when coordinating outfits will help you to put together an executive image that has style and good taste. Become sensitive to these aspects of design, experiment with their use, and you'll soon become your own designer.

EXERCISE

EXERCISE

Go to a store and study an outfit on a mannequin. In a notebook, write down why the outfit goes together according to the elements and principles of design. Do this with several outfits until you're sensitive to these keys to coordination. Now pull together an outfit from your closet. Include accessories and shoes. Write down why you think this outfit goes together according to the elements and principles described in this chapter

EIGHTEEN

The Individual You Are

In this chapter, we'll address some of the unique personal challenges and opportunities you face in developing your executive image.

Women

As we ease the tape measure around our bodies, we generally find that we don't meet with ideal standards. Perhaps our hips are bigger than any other part of our body. Or perhaps our shoulders are extremely broad and out of proportion to the rest of our figure. Clothing is the way to deal with such figure irregularities. Remember, *most* women do not meet an ideal standard. The key is to play up your assets and camouflage your liabilities.

If an ample derriere is your figure flaw, make sure pants fit smoothly and properly. Ill-fitting or tight pants only maximize your problem. Pants should be loose enough over the thighs that the fabric flows smoothly from fanny to leg. Also, avoid tight fitting, box style jackets; they only accentuate your figure flaw. Rather, choose a longer styled jacket, but not too long to shorten your leggy image.

If your derriere is flat, choose styles with fullness in the back such as gathered skirts. Consider layers of fabric in the back to add fullness, or details such as bows. Avoid drop-skirted fashions altogether.

If your thighs are heavy, you are not alone. Heavy thighs are quite common. To camouflage this figure flaw, choose A-line skirts or dresses. Be sure pants and skirts fit correctly, since, again, tight clothing calls attention to the problem. If you like shorts, choose walking or city short styles with or without cuffed bottoms. Cuffs will even out the width in the upper thigh. Avoid short shorts and pants that taper at the ankle; these styles also emphasize heavy thighs.

If your legs are short, avoid cuffed pants. Wear high-heeled shoes and high-waisted styles to give a leggier image. Avoid long skirts, since they also point to your short legs. Instead, wear skirts that fall right at or slightly above the knee.

If your legs are long, avoid high-waisted styles, but do wear pants with cuffs. You might also consider wearing tunics and drop-waisted styles.

If your waist is wide, avoid calling attention to this figure flaw by wearing belts of the same fabric as your dress or narrow belts in similar colors as your clothing. Choose princess, high, or drop-waisted styles. Layered clothing creates a no-waist look and camouflages a wide waist. However, if you're long-waisted, choose wide belts or skirts and pants with high waist bands.

If you have a large bust, avoid sleeves that end at the bust line, high-waisted styles, low yolks, and the use of horizontal lines at the bust. Also stay away from wide belts and belts that are cinched at the waist, since these only emphasize the largeness of the breasts. Wear V-necklines with lapels and vertical lines in printed stripes or in the structural design of the dress or blouse. If you're small busted, on the other hand, choose blousy designs and avoid necklines that expose the cleavage or cling to the skin.

If your shoulders are broad, avoid boat-neck styles and epaulets. Sloping or narrow shoulders benefit from padding at the shoulders and V-neck clothing styles.

If you're petite or average and want to appear taller or longer, emphasize vertical lines in your wardrobe selections. Vertical lines are found in striped fabrics, pleats and other design features, and long chains. Choose high-waisted skirts and trousers and short, waist-length jackets such as the Chanel or Eisenhower styles. Avoid longer hemlines, which make your legs appear shorter; skirts and dresses should be knee-length or a little shorter.

Wear heels, not flats, and consider V-neck styles in blouses. V-necks, combined with vertical design lines, contribute much to your taller image.

Looking Ten Pounds Thinner

So you've gained a few pounds and you want to camouflage the weight while you're reducing—or you just want to appear slimmer. The clothing you wear can help create the illusion of slimness, or certainly minimize the extra weight. Here are some specific tips to incorporate in your wardrobe for a slenderizing appearance.

- Black slenderizes any area. If you are bottom heavy, wear pants or skirts in black and top with patterned or bright-colored blouses. The bright color or pattern draws the eye upward to your face.

- Avoid shiny or heavily textured fabrics. Shiny fabrics reflect light, making any area appear larger. Heavily textured fabrics only add extra weight.

- Incorporate vertical lines. Sewn-down pleats in skirts and blouses and princess seams in a dress can both create a slimming effect. Include vertical lines in your accessories, such as long chains worn around the neck.

- Your best asset is your face, so draw attention to it with scarves and jewelry worn around the face.

- Avoid wearing clothes that have become too tight. These only accentuate your weight. Full silhouettes may cover weight gain, but the extra material adds unnecessary weight.

- Introduce simple lines, such as A-line skirts, tailor-notched, collared blouses, and blazers. The oversized blazer is a great solution for camouflaging large derrieres and hips. Double-pleated skirts and trousers mask protruding stomachs and provide comfort as well.

- Emphasize angular, as opposed to rounded, shapes and styles in your wardrobe. Angular shapes offset the roundness of the body and bring it into balance.

■ Avoid extensive use of horizontal lines—belts, boat-collar blouses, and border print skirts. These styles can add extra width to your body frame.

■ If you have large legs, try dark hose. Off-black, charcoal, taupe, black, and coffee will all make legs appear thinner, while white, pearl, and cream will have the opposite effect. And choose sheer hosiery rather than opaque stockings or tights. You want a hint of color rather than a covered appearance.

Men

Yes, men have figure flaws too. Many of the same rules apply to you as to women, with some additions. If you're frustrated when you shop because you don't know what to look for, these tips will help you bring out your individuality!

■ If you are on the short side and want to appear taller, purchase suits with vertical pin or chalk stripes. Consider three-button suits, either solid or pin-striped. Avoid plaid, tweed, and double-breasted jackets, which add width rather than height. You want to have a continuing vertical line from head to toe, so your pants should be hemmed to create only a slight break in the trouser as the pant front rests on the shoe. Trousers and shoes should be closely matched to each other and to the jacket to enhance the continuous, unbroken line to the floor.

■ If you want to minimize your height, emphasize horizontal lines. Try plaid patterns and double-breasted jackets. Consider a jacket in one color, such as navy, and trousers in another, such as gray or khaki. Cuffed pants subtract inches as well.

■ If you're on the heavy side and want to appear slimmer, choose dark-colored and/or pin and chalk striped suits. Double-breasted suits with closely spaced buttons can be slimming, as can trim sweaters with set-in sleeves and V necklines. Avoid bulky sweaters, unstructured jackets, and items with lots of horizontal lines and extra details, such as pant pockets down the leg.

- If you want to appear heavier, consider tweeds, glen plaids, scotch, tartan, or madras plaids, corduroy, wool flannel (for winter), and linen and cotton (for summer). Introduce pleated pants, bulky sweaters, warmer, brighter colors, and whites to your wardrobe. Consider also double-breasted jackets, square-shoulder, European-cut, and double-vented suit styles. Avoid fabrics that cling to the skin, like lightweight silks and nylon shirts, and consider padded shoulders in suits, shirts, and sweaters. Emphasize horizontal stripes in sweaters and shirts.

- If your shoulders are wider than your hips, consider double pleated pants. Wearing pants in colors lighter than your shirt, or in heavier fabrics like corduroy, denim, linen, and canvas, also helps. Jackets with patch pockets also add width to the hip area.

- If your hips are the same or wider than your shoulders, emphasize the shoulders and chest. Choose bulky sweaters, shirts with epaulets, and heavier shirt fabrics like pinpoint oxford cloth, heavy cottons, and linen. Choose shirts with a lot of details, shirts with horizontal stripes, or two-toned shirts with a lighter color in the yoke area. Avoid pleated pants in favor of plain, emphasizing dark colors like navy, charcoal gray, charcoal brown, olive, and black.

- If your legs are short, avoid cuffed pants. Choose pants with vertical lines, such as corduroy or pin or chalk stripes. Hem pants so that there's only a slight break in the pant front. Three-button suits also add the illusion of length.

- If your legs are long, go ahead and wear cuffs. Purchase suit jackets that are slightly longer than usual, with one or two button closings. Choose contrasting colors for shirts and pants.

- If your shoulders are extremely sloped, choose jackets with padding. Avoid raglan sleeves in sweaters and shirts, since they emphasize or follow the slope of the shoulder. Instead, choose set-in sleeves and jacket lapels that point upward. Avoid unstructured jackets altogether.

- If your shoulders are square, do consider raglan sleeve sweaters. Avoid extremes in lapel width; these tend to call attention to the shoulder area. Choose unstructured jackets or suits with natural shoulders.

EXERCISE

EXERCISE

First, take an honest look at yourself in a full length mirror and note your body proportions. What are your height/weight and shoulder/hip proportions? Are your shoulders straight and broad or sloped and narrow? Are you short or long-waisted? Are your legs long or short? Examine the proportions of your waist, torso, and legs to determine whether one area seems short and another long. Compare your shoulder width with the width of your hips. Are your hips wider than your shoulders?

Second, with the help of a close friend and a tape measure, measure yourself. Women, wear either a body stocking or bra and panties; men, an undershirt and briefs. Stand with the soles of your feet flat on the floor. Jot down your measurements in the space provided and analyze your figure assets and liabilities. Take this information with you when you shop.

Women

Measure across the bust, waist, and hips (fullest part). Next measure from the top of the head to the bust, from the bust to the fullest part of the hip, from the hip to the middle of the kneecap, and from the kneecap to the floor. Also measure your neck length and the diameter of your wrist and ankle. Note your height and weight. Observe the shape of your shoulders. Are they broad and straight (no slope), broad and tapered (slight sloped), medium and tapered, or medium and sloped (extreme slope)? Record your measurements.

To determine whether you are short or long-waisted, use this rule: The measurement from your bust to your hip and your hip to your knee ideally should be the same. If your bust-to-hip measurement is longer than your hip-to-knee measurement, you are long-waisted. If it is shorter, you are short-waisted and probably have long legs. To further determine leg length, the rule is that the measurement from your head to your bust and from your knee to the sides of your feet should be about the same. If the head-to-bust measurement is shorter than the knee-to-feet measurement, you probably have long legs. However, if this measurement is longer but your hip-to-knee measurement is shorter than your bust-to-hip, you probably have high hips, short thighs, and long calves. Although the 36" 22" 36" figure of the sixties is no longer the standard, bust and hip measurement should be about the same, while the waist should be approximately eight to ten inches smaller. Upper thighs should be about the same measurement as the waist.

Men

Measure yourself at the chest, the fullest part of the hip, and the waist. Also measure across the back at the shoulders, your neck length and diameter, and the diameter of your wrist and ankle. Take the length from the top of your head to the middle of the chest, from the chest to the fullest part of the hip, and from the hip to the middle of the knee to the floor. Note your height and weight. Also note the shape and width of your shoulders. Are they broad and square, broad and tapered (with a slight slope), medium and tapered, or medium and sloped (extreme slope)?

The distance from the top of your head to your chest should ideally equal the distance from the middle of the kneecap to the soles of the feet. The length from the middle of the chest to the fullest part of the hip and from the fullest part of the hip to the middle of the kneecap should likewise be equal. Variations of these length will determine whether you are short or long-waisted and whether you have short or long legs. An average drop in inches from the middle of the chest to the waist is seven inches. That means that the waist should be approximately seven inches smaller than the chest measurement. If you have a greater drop, you probably have an athletic build.

EXERCISE

Women:

Bust:	Length from top of head to bust:
Waist:	Length from bust to fullest part of hips:
Hips:	Length from hips to middle of knee:
Height:	Length from knee to soles of feet:
Weight:	Neck length:
Wrist:	Shape of shoulders:
Ankle:	

My figure assets are:

....
....
....

My figure liabilities are:

....
....
....

Men:

Chest:	Length from top of head to chest:
Waist:	Length from chest to fullest part of hips:
Hips:	Length from hips to middle of knee:
Height:	Length from knee to soles of feet:
Weight:	Neck length:
Wrist:	Shape of shoulders:
Ankle:	Back measurement at shoulders:

My figure assets are:

....
....
....

My figure liabilities are:

....
....
....

EXERCISE

Characteristics	Do Wear	Don't Wear
Long-Waisted	✓ Belts to match skirt or pants ✓ Cummerbund belts	✗ Skinny sweater or top
Protruding Abdomen	✓ A-lines ✓ Sewn-down pleats ✓ Empire waist ✓ Side-slash pockets ✓ Gathers at side of skirt front	✗ Clingy fabrics ✗ Dirndl skirts ✗ Loose pleats ✗ Straight skirts ✗ Snug waistbands ✗ Tight belts
Wide Hips	✓ Fake button placket down	✗ Straight skirts and pants, unless top covers rear ✗ Pocket detail ✗ Jackets that cover whole hip area if you are short (5'3" and under) ✗ Pleated pants, skirts ✗ Back pockets ✗ Big plaids ✗ Horizontal patterns ✗ Bias-cut skirts
Tiny Waist and Large Hips	✓ Narrow loose belt ✓ A-line dresses	✗ Clothes that emphasize tiny waist

Characteristics	Do Wear	Don't Wear
No Hips	✓ Full skirts ✓ Pants that fit sleekly ✓ Loose overshirt ✓ Bulky fabrics	
Flat Rear End	✓ Two-piece outfits with overlapping tops ✓ Trousers altered to fit ✓ Gathered skirts ✓ Pants that fit smoothly	
Bowlegs	✓ Longer skirts ✓ Soft full skirts ✓ A-line skirts ✓ Full-cut slacks	✗ Straight Skirts
Short Legs	✓ High-waisted pants ✓ Corduroy pants ✓ Three-button suit	✗ Pants with cuffs
Long Neck	✓ Shirts with collars ✓ White or light-colored turtlenecks	✗ V-Neck sweaters, shirts and blouses ✗ Scoopneck shirts, blouses and sweaters
Pointed Chin	✓ Rounded collars	✗ V-Necks
Long Legs	✓ Pants with cuffs ✓ Contrasting colors for shirts and pants ✓ Suit jackets that are slightly longer, with one to two button closings	✗ High-waisted styles ✗ Vertical patterns in pants

Characteristics	Do Wear	Don't Wear
Tall and Thin	✓ Bulky sweaters ✓ Fluffy wools, thick sweaters ✓ Fur ✓ Voile ✓ Gauze ✓ Boots ✓ Blouson waists ✓ Soft cowl necklines ✓ Full graceful sleeves ✓ Full skirts ✓ 2 or 3 piece outfits in contrasting colors ✓ Plaids ✓ Double-breasted jackets ✓ Padded shoulders in suits and shirts ✓ Square-shouldered suits ✓ White and other light-colored clothing	✗ Vertically striped patterns ✗ Heavy shoes ✗ Tapered shirts ✗ Dark solids ✗ Fabrics that cling
Short	✓ One-tone or one-color suit in cool colors ✓ Delicate high heeled shoes ✓ Slim-line skirt ✓ Vertical patterns in pinstripes ✓ Vertical seaming ✓ Slim-line slacks ✓ Three-button suits	✗ Bulky, complicated clothing ✗ Cluttered neckline ✗ Skirt too long or too short ✗ Ankle strap shoes ✗ Thick-soled or heavy shoes ✗ Plaids ✗ Tweeds ✗ Double-breasted jackets

Characteristics	Do Wear	Don't Wear
Large Figure	✓ Clothing that fits well ✓ Well-tailored dark suits ✓ Cloths that accent the face (bows, ties, printed shirts) ✓ Solid colors ✓ Smooth fabrics ✓ Pin or chalk-striped suits ✓ Tops and shirts outside the skirt or trousers ✓ Narrow belt pushed down a bit further that normal ✓ Blouson tops ✓ Light-colored shirts with belt lighter than pants	✗ Skintight or very loose garments ✗ Bold patterns ✗ Front-pleated trousers ✗ Pleated or dirndl skirts ✗ Large plaids ✗ Bulky sweaters ✗ Unstructured jackets ✗ Colors that change at waist ✗ Wide belts
Wide Shoulders	**To de-emphasize:** ✓ Garments with shoulder seams slightly within real shoulder line ✓ Soft fabrics ✓ Silky blouses gathered at yolk ✓ Raglan sleeves ✓ Double-pleated pants	**To emphasize:** ✗ Cap sleeves ✗ Dolman sleeves ✗ Sleeveless garments ✗ Stiff fabrics ✗ Horizontal stripes ✗ Light-colored sweaters ✗ Bold bright colors ✗ Bulky sweaters ✗ Heavier shirting fabrics such as pinpoint, oxford, and denim ✗ Plain front pants

PART THREE:
ETIQUETTE: PERSONAL SAVVY
FOR SUCCESS

Etiquette—
A Lost Art

WHEN IT COMES TO ETIQUETTE, many aspiring executives receive A's in skills but D's on approach, which inhibits promotability to the top. Perhaps you've heard your boss tell you

you're "rough around the edges." Look around at some of the successful executives in your office. You'll notice they have a polished air, that they're well connected, approachable, and polite. They have mastered the art of corporate etiquette.

When we think of etiquette, visions of charm school float to the surface. But etiquette is not charm school; it's a set of guidelines for everyday living. Living ethically means respecting those around you. If we all practiced etiquette, I believe that the world would be a kinder, more thoughtful place to live.

By mastering this art, you, too, can project the polished image of an executive. This part of the book is designed to increase your level of confidence in unfamiliar situations. When you feel self-assured, you will be free to devote your mind to other concerns like making deals or establishing new connections.

This section of the book is by no means an exhaustive look at the subject of etiquette. After all, many thick volumes have been devoted solely to etiquette. If you find yourself wanting to know more, you are certainly encouraged to take advantage of them. However, what is covered in the next ten chapters captures the essence of everyday etiquette. It should help you put your best foot forward in business and social situations.

A lot has changed over the years in our society, including standards of appropriate behavior. One of the greatest changes influencing etiquette has been women working. Gentlemanly behavior is still in demand—but not at the office. A man pulling out a chair for a woman could be in big trouble. And who opens the door these days, men or women? Often it's the junior executive, male or female. Other times it's whoever gets to the door first.

Yes, some things have changed, especially the roles of men and women. However, some things haven't. In the following pages, we'll look at etiquette for the '90s and beyond in a variety of situations.

NINETEEN

Introductions

Introductions are crucial. Why? Because when you are meeting someone for the first time, you have about four minutes to make the impression that you are confident, knowledgeable, warm and personable—someone the person you are meeting can trust to do business with or get to know further.

There is something funny going on in our society these days. No one introduces anyone anymore. It seems you have to fend for yourself, whether you are at a large function or a meeting. If you learn nothing else from this section of the book, remember to introduce people. If you don't get in the habit of introducing people, your trip up the corporate ladder may well be jeopardized.

Introductions are crucial from a social as well as a business standpoint. They bring two people together to exchange business information or enhance their networks. So make a point of introducing people you know at parties, meetings, the company picnic, wherever. You will be remembered kindly for it.

Who should be introduced to whom? The basic rules for introductions are:

1. Introduce a man to a woman: "Ms. Smith, I would like to introduce to you Mr. Jones."
2. Introduce a younger person to an older person.

3. Introduce an individual of lower rank or status to an individual of higher rank or status.
4. Introduce a person you know less to a person you know more.
5. Introduce a peer in your own company to a peer in another company.
6. Introduce a fellow executive to a customer or client.
7. Introduce a nonofficial person to an official person.

When introducing people of similar ages, don't try to figure out who's older; just do it. During the introduction you should give the introductee's last name and some information about him or her to ignite conversation. A good starter is to mention something that the two people have in common. It is not customary to mention the introductee's work unless it's something interesting and what he loves to do. If you introduce Bob to Sheri and say that Bob is an accountant, Sheri might continue this flow by saying, "What a fascinating job," causing Bob to reply, "No it isn't," and walk off. Instead, mention something that will carry the conversation forward and stimulate interaction between the two, such as hobbies or travels.

When introducing people, don't make wisecracks like, "This is Bob, he's into toilets," when he's really a plumber. There's really nothing ruder than making wisecracks about someone's work. It's important to be genuine when introducing people.

When you are introduced and your last name is not mentioned in the introduction, say it when you greet the new person. For example, "Sheri, I would like to introduce to you Bob; he's working on a book about the relationship between art and literature in the sixteenth century." "How do you do, I'm Sheri Walker." "I'm Bob Smith, and it's a pleasure to meet you."

When you're at a party or a meeting and your group is joined by someone only you know, you must take the responsibility of introducing him or her to the others. To do this, you should interrupt the group's conversation and say something like, "Dick, it's great to see you! I'd like to introduce my associates at XYZ—Lynda Smith, Katie Todd, Bob Anderson, and Sue Thomas. And this is Dick Marlin, a newcomer to Los Angeles, who recently joined the law firm of Andrews & Thomas."

One of the common mistakes people make is to avoid introducing someone they know because they happen to have forgotten his or her name. Please don't let a memory lapse stop you. How do you get around it? There are several ways. First, admit your human frailty: "Gosh, I've forgotten your name, how stupid of me," or "I have your name on the tip of my tongue, but I just can't seem to get it past there." Don't apologize a thousand times—it just focuses attention on your error. The second way around it is to tell an ego-boosting story about the person. Hopefully, the other people around you will ask for his or her name, which the person will probably supply happily. If someone has obviously forgotten your name, don't make them guess. Give your name quickly, first and last, and they will appreciate you much more for helping them out.

If you have a habit of forgetting names, you may want to practice a few simple techniques. When a friend introduces someone—"Mary, I'd like you to meet Bob Marks"—repeat the person's name in your head, then repeat it again out loud when you greet him: "It's a pleasure to meet you, Mr. Marks." Then find a word association to tie the name with the face. In business, and when hosting of a party, remembering names is a must; people are always appreciative when you remember their name.

If you see someone you want to meet and no one has taken the time to introduce you, why not introduce yourself? It's a fearful thought, but really not all that painful to do. Almost everyone wants to meet new people, and it is considered perfectly appropriate to go ahead and introduce yourself. But how do you do it with minimal pain and maximum success? One thing that you can remember when deciding whether to introduce yourself is that friends were once strangers who either were introduced by a mutual friend or introduced themselves to each other.

When you approach someone, be direct, honest, genuine, positive, and personable. Most people are attracted to someone who is warm, friendly, and on the up-and-up. One way to introduce yourself is to identify a common ground or give a compliment. For example, "I really love the color of that suit—it looks great on you; by the way, I'm Susan Haywood," or, "I notice you're from Iowa. I'm from Iowa. What city do you live in? By the way, I'm Karen Jackson." Whatever you say, be sincere. People just hate, "Don't I know you from somewhere?" That entry will surely end in failure. If you know you've met the person somewhere and you know where, then say it. "We met at the American Business Women's convention in Las Vegas last November during the social hour; I'm Barbara Smith." That will turn the light on rather than off.

If the introduction falls through, the worst you could feel is a little heartache or lost pride—no permanent damage. Life is composed of degrees of risk. But what if you're successful? If you fail the first time, keep trying. In between the failures will be successes and lots of new acquaintances.

When introducing people or yourself, there is always the concern about titles and first names. How do you introduce your friend the former mayor to one of your associates? Do you call him mayor? What are the rules?

When introducing someone, you should use that person's designated title. For example, "Mr. Mayor, I would like to introduce to you Dr. Jones." You use the designated title even if the person is retired. If the person is a retired colonel, you still say, "Colonel Bowling, I would like to introduce to you Judge Smith."

As a point of interest, this rule also holds true for the current or former president of the United States. The proper way to introduce a man or a woman to the president is, "Mr. President, I have the honor of presenting Mr. Bruce Williams of Kansas City." This rule also applies to members of the Senate and House of Representatives. "Mrs. Williams, I would like to introduce to you Senator Jones."

When introducing a woman, unless she is a medical doctor, a holder of a doctorate degree, or a judge, you'll want to use the title "Ms." unless otherwise notified. This will save you a lot of embarrassment. "Ms./Dr. Jones, I would like to introduce to you Jack Haywood."

How about first names? A lot of people are confused about using someone's first name in an introduction or while conversing with him. When are they used and when are they not used?

The best rule of thumb is, if you have to think about whether to call someone by his first name, don't. You will save yourself a lot of turmoil if you introduce him by his correct title or by his first and last name. Most people who have earned a position in life appreciate the respect given to their status; if you refuse to call attention to it they will most certainly be offended. Even if the person answers, "Call me Jack," you'll start off on a better foot if you respect his position and introduce him by his title and last name. By the same token, a person with an earned doctorate should be called "Doctor," although he or she may opt for Mr., Mrs., or Ms. during social hours.

Other rules of thumb regarding the use of first names are as follows. A younger person should wait for an older person to ask before using her first name. A junior executive should wait for a senior executive to ask. Just because an older or more senior person calls you by your first name doesn't mean you can call her by her first name. Even if she requests that you call her by her first name, use her title or her first and last name when introducing her to other people. A less official person should also wait for a more official person to ask.

When children are introduced to or refer to an adult other than one of their parents, they should call the adult by his or her title, Dr., Mr., Mrs., or Ms., and the adult's last name, unless directed otherwise by the person in question. You should also be sure to use a person's last name in his or her absence when the people present may not know who you are referring to.

There are certain circumstances under which introductions are not appropriate. One is when you are in a public place where it's hard to hear and conversation is not likely. Another is when you know that the two people don't want to meet. Perhaps your friend feels strongly about saving the animals and the other is wearing a fur. These two people should probably not be introduced, to prevent a quarrel from taking place.

EXERCISE

Practice introducing people, using your friends and relatives until you feel comfortable. Then, at least once a week, introduce people using the information presented in the chapter. Also practice introducing yourself, again using your family or friends to build confidence. Then, at least once a week, introduce yourself to someone new, perhaps at an association meeting or in another department where you work. You'll gain a whole new circle of peers as a result.

TWENTY

Greetings

Once you've been introduced, what then? As stated earlier, one person can size up another in three to four seconds. However, in the four minutes after a first meeting you have the opportunity to make or break those formed expectations, beginning with your greeting. The first impression is a lasting one, so it's important to consider not only how you look but your body language and appropriate behavior. Once you've been introduced, what do you say, or better yet, what do you do, to put your best foot forward?

When you are introduced, if you are seated, stand up. This communicates that you are indeed happy to meet the person. Remaining seated says that you are not interested in him and that you are probably not worth knowing either.

Once you have stood up, step forward and smile. Even if it's been a tough day, try to look pleasant. Then extend your hand and give your name. It is important to maintain eye contact as you do this. Once you've given your name, repeat the other person's name: "Hello, I'm John Doe; it's a pleasure to meet you, Mr. Smith." If you don't get the correct pronunciation of the person's name, ask him to pronounce it again. "Excuse me, could you please say your name again? I want to know it." "Hi," is an informal greeting reserved for someone you already know. In business, "Good morning," or "Good afternoon" after lunch, is more appropriate.

When you are in public and someone sees you and says hello, a smile and a nod is all that's needed when passing by. Sometimes, and this happens to all of us, you will be greeted by someone you do not recognize, perhaps because the person is in different clothing. It's still better to nod and acknowledge such a greeting than to be thought of as rude.

The handshake is the most common form of greeting in the United States and England. It has been used as a form of greeting for hundreds of years, originally signaling an agreement. The handshake is a must for women as well as men. If a man extends his hand, a woman must shake it. Not to do so would be taken as unfriendly.

When a man is introduced to a woman outside of business circumstances, the lady has the right to choose whether to extend her hand. If she does offer her hand, the man should shake it. When children are introduced to adults, they, too, should shake hands.

Shake hands when saying hello or goodbye. When someone enters your office from the outside, you should stand and shake hands. You should also shake hands when you run into someone outside the office. At a party, shake the host's hand when arriving and the host's and recent acquaintances' hands when leaving.

When being introduced to someone who does not have full use of his or her right arm, extend your right hand anyway. The person will appreciate that you have not tried to adjust to his predicament and will probably extend the left hand to shake.

A good handshake is essential to making the right impression. A lot can be learned about you through your handshake. A hearty handshake gives the impression that you are personable, positive, and really glad to meet the new person. A lifeless handshake suggests a lifeless person.

There are correct and incorrect ways of shaking hands. Incorrect includes the handshake that cripples the hand and the notorious "limp fish." Another style of handshake, often associated with politicians, is what some call the "politician's pump" or "the glove." The person in question, who meets many people, holds out his right hand with a big smile and grabs your right forearm or covers your right hand during the shake. This style usually turns people off in a first meeting. Save it for old friends.

What is a good handshake? One that is positive and firm and held for about three or four seconds. You should give direct eye contact and smile during this time.

Some people prefer to hug and kiss when greeting one another. This greeting is common in places like Brazil, but not in the United States, where hugging and kissing should be abstained from in public or business settings. When seeing an old friend you can extend your right hand and grab his arm or shoulder with your left. When male and female business associates see each other, they should not kiss at all. It sends rumors flying.

If you tend to be nervous when meeting people, resulting in clammy hands, don't fret. Carry a handkerchief with you and wipe them off before meeting someone. If you are at a cocktail party and your hands are damp from your glass, mention this when meeting someone and immediately wipe them off. You might say, "I'm sorry about my wet hand." Given how common this predicament is at cocktail parties, you might want to consider holding your drink in your left hand to save yourself the embarrassment. Or consider placing a cocktail napkin between your hand and the glass.

Once we've safely passed the greeting, how do we initiate conversation? You could ask the person how she's feeling or make a comment about the weather, but these topics may not get you far. What are some interesting approaches to conversation? Well, you could try learning more about the person—where she comes from, what she does for a living, and so on. A word of caution, though: your new acquaintance may feel this is "twenty questions," and recoil. Go easy with this approach. The point is to find an area that creates rapport between the two of you, not a one-sided conversation. Try to ask questions that can't be answered with yes or no. You want to establish some commonality between the two of you as well as seek information about the other person. If you ask her what she does for a living, pursue a rapport by asking what her job entails, what is exciting about it, or what she has done in the past to prepare for this occupation. The important thing is to be interested!

Another way to get past the hellos and how-do-you-do's is to ask questions related to attitudes, likes, and dislikes. If you're at a cocktail party, you might ask about the food, the music, or the place it's being held. Or you might ask whether your new acquaintance has an interest in the arts. Learning about someone's likes and dislikes is an important part of the total impression of the person you're meeting.

Another way to stimulate rapport is to volunteer information about yourself. If you've moved recently, you could mention where you came from and the differences you found between your former home and your new one. With any luck, the other person will be compelled to tell of a similar move or travels and the differences noted between the two. If the new acquaintance volunteers information that can be helpful to you such as a service or product that she provides, you'll gain a lot of ground. Perhaps she will see it as an opportunity to gain a new client and dive into the conversation.

Another way to stimulate rapport after you've been introduced is to give a compliment. If you're going to give one, however, be sincere. The new person will usually react positively to your compliment and return it with a "thank you." When this is a sincere gesture, the compliment approach can be the easiest way to establish rapport. Compliments can have sexual overtones, particularly when members of the opposite sex meet, but this approach can introduce a mutual admiration between the two if it is not overdone. A man may make a compliment about a woman's jewelry, dress, or hair, but should, or course, refrain from saying, "You have a great body" or anything vaguely similar. A woman might also give a compliment to a man about his clothing or suntan. Refrain from saying, "You have beautiful eyes."

Another way of establishing rapport during the greeting is to identify common interests or acquaintances. For example, you might start out, "Hello, my name is Susan Martin, and I noticed from your jacket emblem that you went to Harvard. I went there too. What did you study?" Some other areas in common might include the fact that your children go to the same high school or are on the cheerleading squad together. Or you may have mutual associates from the past or currently. The common ground might be your aspirations and goals in life, your club memberships, and so on. Whatever it is, grasp this mutual knowledge and use it to establish a rapport.

Humor is another approach: "Gosh, if this party gets any more populated, we'll have to start lining up like sardines." Avoid off-color jokes and other touchy subjects. It's safer to joke about the weather rather than about religion, race, politics, or the battle of the sexes, all topics that could strike a sour chord with your new acquaintance. Use your best judgment, and keep in mind what your abilities are. If your jokes never get laughed at, you might want to veer away from this approach, which will only make you appear awkward.

Another way to approach someone is to start a conversation about your hobbies. If one of your hobbies is traveling, you might ask whether the other person has traveled and talk about his experiences. Or mention something about your recent travels. Remember, this is your hobby, so don't monopolize the conversation. Instead, ask him about his hobbies. Now both of you are talking about subjects you love. While he is telling you about his hobby, make sure you at least look interested. Ask questions. This brings out the best in people and establishes a sound, lasting rapport.

Asking for help is another way of establishing rapport. "I want to determine the best investment for my dollars for retirement; could you enlighten me on what might be the best direction to go?" People are more than happy to help someone who asks for advice. But don't give unsolicited advice; no one wants that. If you're in a new town, asking for information is a great way to get to know people in the community. Who is the best family practitioner? Where should you go for a great meal and entertainment? Who is the best veterinarian? These are just starters.

Another approach is the one where the other person reminds you of someone. This is touchy, because it's been abused. Men have been known to say this to women they're interested in just to break the ice, when in actuality there was no resemblance whatsoever.

You might approach someone in an apologetic manner, though not in such a way as to give the impression that you consider yourself worthless. Rather, you might mention something about the fact that you're dressed inappropriately for a dinner party, or the reason why you were late, or that you're not familiar with a topic of conversation. Again, this approach requires grace. You don't want someone to think you don't value yourself.

These are just some of the many ways to establish rapport with another person. The important thing to remember is to be sincere and interested in the person you're meeting.

EXERCISE

EXERCISE

Practice your handshake until you feel comfortable with it. In the weeks that
follow, experiment with each of the approaches described in this chapter to
create rapport between you and new acquaintances. How do they react? Do
these approaches stimulate rapport? Determine which you feel comfortable
with. Use the following guide to record your observations.

Week: ....

1st approach:

....
....
....

Was it successful? Why or why not?

....
....
....

2nd approach:

....
....
....

Was it successful? Why or why not?

....
....
....

3rd approach:

....
....
....

Was it successful? Why or why not?

....
....
....

Week: ....

4th approach:

....

....

....

Was it successful? Why or why not?

....

....

....

5th approach:

....

....

....

Was it successful? Why or why not?

....

....

....

6th approach:

....

....

....

Was it successful? Why or why not?

....

....

....

EXERCISE

EXERCISE

Week: ....

7th approach:

....
....
....

Was it successful? Why or why not?

....
....
....

8th approach:

....
....
....

Was it successful? Why or why not?

....
....
....

Which of the approaches seemed consistent with your personality?

....
....
....

Which do you feel comfortable about using in the future?

....
....
....

TWENTY-ONE

The Art of Good Conversation

Have you ever met someone you found fun and interesting to talk to? Can you recall being introduced to someone and becoming instantly engrossed in conversation?

Fun and interesting people have a grasp of good conversational skills. On the other hand, have you ever felt inadequate to survive a cocktail party, showing up only to find yourself alone? Have you ever been introduced to someone who just didn't have anything to talk about or who gave you only yes or no answers to your questions?

Learning to be a good conversationalist is relatively easy, if you equip yourself with the right ammunition. Good conversational ability can take you a long way in life. People remember those they enjoyed conversing with. Being a good conversationalist makes a lasting impression with the people you meet and with your employer.

Today it seems that there are a lot of wallflowers out there who are frozen stiff when it comes to conversation. Many others can only talk about their work or themselves. These conversational misfits lack essential skills, skills that can alter the impression they make on others.

Good conversation is a process of give and take. Good conversationalists don't pretend to know more than they know. If you don't know what the other person is talking about, don't pretend you do. Use the opportunity to ask questions and stimulate discussion.

Good conversationalists think before they speak, taking time to put together their thoughts. They are also sensitive to the signals sent by their audience, whether one person or a roomful. They are aware when they are boring their audience or are touching on a subject that is too sensitive to others.

Good conversationalists are good listeners. Listening to others is probably more important in conversation than what you say. Some consider listening a passive act, but in fact it is just the opposite. It is a product of the mind more than just the ears. Listening requires that you absorb what is being said, looking at the person who is speaking and sending a signal of attention. You must actively grasp the speaker's words and interpret them in your own world. All of these traits should be pursued when listening to others.

There are few things more annoying than talking to someone who begins to give signs that he is not listening. You're probably familiar with these signs: turning away from the speaker, avoiding eye contact, hair playing or other nervous habits, and talking before the person speaking is finished. This is not only frustrating to the speaker but outright rude. It makes you want to grab the person you're speaking to and say "Listen to me!"

To help you learn to listen more effectively, follow these suggestions:

- Repeat in your mind, word by word, what the other person is saying.
- Keep eye contact with him or her while he or she is speaking.
- Face him or her with your body.
- Wait until he or she is finished talking before you speak.
- Paraphrase or summarize what was just said.
- Ask questions.

When you sense your mind wandering to chores not yet done or to a new business deal, start to repeat everything the other person says in your mind. This will direct your full attention back to the speaker. Effective listening is a skill that must be practiced daily. An effective listener is a delight to others.

A good conversationalist is aware of the world around him and knowledgeable about many topics. This is not to suggest that you go out and try to master higher physics; however, you should be aware of and be able to carry on a light conversation about a variety of topics. Someone who can only talk shop (or business) is boring to others. Just being aware of the world around you is enough to make you a more interesting conversationalist.

One way to become aware of current events is to read, watch, or listen to the news each day. Listening to the news while getting ready for work is an easy way to keep abreast of current events. Books, plays, movies, and music also make good topics for conversation. A good conversationalist takes the time and effort to learn about different topics.

Good conversationalists do not monopolize the conversation. In particular they don't fasten on the word "I." One of the quickest turn-offs is a person who won't quit talking about what he is doing. Such a person is probably insecure. Try to get the new acquaintance to talk about herself, and be cautious not to talk a lot about yourself.

Good conversationalists don't burst someone's bubble with put-downs or corrections. If someone mispronounces your name upon introduction, you can say it in the correct way by replying, "Pleased to meet you, I'm Harry Seitz." But if the person uses the wrong verb tense, don't point it out. It's not your place. Nor is it your place to put other people down. If someone exaggerates while telling a story, that's her problem, not yours. Overlook these weaknesses graciously.

Good conversationalists include everyone in the conversation, not just one or two. Furthermore, they try to make shy people feel welcome. If you're at a party when someone comes in and the host is not able to get to him, welcome him to your conversation circle.

A good conversationalist doesn't gossip or use vulgarity. Gossip is just that, gossip. It shows disrespect for the person you're talking about, the people you're talking to, and yourself. If you don't want others to talk behind your back, then don't participate in talking behind their backs.

A good conversationalist avoids vulgarity. Vulgar language reflects a lack of vocabulary skills and has no place in business or social settings. It's not okay for men to use vulgar terminology when describing something that happened to them, nor is it okay for women to use vulgarity in their speech. The constant use of vulgarity is invariably distasteful, and not appreciated by others around you. Try to find other words to describe your feelings.

A good conversationalist gives and receives compliments gracefully. How often have you paid a compliment to someone and gotten a dissertation in response? Maybe you said that the person had a beautiful dress on and they described the whole shopping experience as well as the sale price.

When you pay a compliment, it should be sincere. People can tell if you're trying to impress them or win them over to your side with your compliment. If you can't pay a sincere one, don't pay one at all. Furthermore, if you're always paying compliments others will eventually begin to discount them. You'll lose credibility.

A good conversationalist is interested in what other people do for a living and takes pleasure in their good news and good fortune. If you can't be glad at a colleague's good fortune for some reason, then don't say anything.

When you meet someone who has chosen a different career path from yours, act interested in what he does. Ask questions about his job—its responsibilities, its opportunities, and what it takes to get hired. (Refrain from asking his salary. That is not acceptable.) Listen carefully: in the years ahead things and situations may change and you might be looking for a new career. Learning about others' occupations may show the way to future opportunities.

There are some topics and behaviors that need to be avoided when you are practicing the art of conversation. For example, when someone starts to talk about her problems, don't give unsolicited advice. Such a person usually just wants an attentive ear. When someone asks for advice, if you are knowledgeable in the area, go ahead and advise, but if not, don't put yourself in the position of expert. Just admit that you don't know. There's no shame in that. And remember, when someone does ask for your advice, don't give the whole encyclopedia of wise thoughts; just offer a little at a time. Sharing a similar experience is probably the best route to go.

Don't question someone you have just met as if you're conducting an interrogation. Phrase your questions so that you can seem to be interested in the person.

Silence is golden, but conversation is give-and-take. Someone who always listens, never giving any feedback, is boring. Yes, it's important to listen effectively; however, part of conversation is responding to the person who was talking. Don't interrupt someone while he is speaking, but return his remarks with questions, by paraphrasing what he just said, or by acknowledging what was said with a nod.

Some other rules that a good conversationalist will master are as follows:

- If the conversation is going well, don't change the subject.
- Don't point the conversation in your direction constantly; give others the opportunity to share.
- When in the presence of celebrities or noted authorities, don't make wisecracks or ask about other famous people; celebrities have earned their stardom. If you try to take their limelight away, you will usually be seen as foolish.
- Don't talk about matters that should be confidential. When you do, you give others the green light to spread the word.
- Be sensitive to the use of filler words like "um" and the repetition of phrases like "you know."
- Strive for clarity so that others don't have to translate what you say. In other words, communicate—don't miscommunicate.

What topics and questions should one avoid in conversation?

- First and foremost, don't ask questions or discuss personal topics like your health, someone else's health, yours or someone else's sex life, yours or someone else's age, and/or whether someone is going through therapy. Similarly, you should refrain from asking someone's weight or shoe size, whether the person is wearing a wig or toupee, whether that's a real diamond, what the person's sexual preference is, how his or her divorce or chemotherapy is going, or whether he or she has been laid off.
- Don't ask or tell how much things cost. You can go to a realtor, dealer, or store for that information. Someone who is always talking about money—how much they have or don't have—is boring.
- Don't share personal misfortunes; however, if someone wants to share his, be a good listener.
- Don't talk about sensitive subjects like religion, politics, or abortion among recent acquaintances or those you know to be sensitive on

such issues. If you want to avoid starting an all-out drag-out fight or spoiling a new acquaintance, stay off the touchy subjects. Besides, talking about something that has been covered over and over again in the news will only bore your audience.

What do you talk about? Starting a conversation with someone when you are at dinner, in a taxi cab, or in any other situation can be difficult if you don't know what to talk about. Small talk is the best answer for such situations. In social settings it can lead to more serious discussions, but otherwise it's the filler between meetings, before meetings, or on the way to the airport. Here are a few topics you could consider using:

- Information about the performing arts, like plays, the symphony, the opera, concerts, and art festivals. Maybe you've seen a great new play—spread the word!
- The environment. Talk about recycling issues, growth of forests, and cleaning the air and water. (This may be a sensitive issue with some people, so feel them out before diving in.)
- New developments in science. This usually gets a positive response. Talk about new discoveries in medicine and other areas of science.
- The Olympics. Where are they going to be held? Which events will be the most exciting this time? When do they begin? (They are staggered in such a way as to occur every two years, with winter and summer games two years apart.)
- News about the competition. This is a good topic to mention when you're with your boss. It shows that you're astute and aware.
- Gardening. This is a hobby many people indulge in on the weekends. You can also talk about sports and other hobbies.
- Bestselling books and top movies. Be sure that you've read the books or seen the movies before talking about them. You might spur small talk by asking what the bestsellers are.
- If you're at a dinner party, you may want to mention to the person seated next to you something positive about the evening, such as how good the food or music is.
- If you run into someone you've met before, mention something about a mutual friend.

■ If you're at a party and just can't think of anything to say, say something neutral about current events, or compliment them on what they're wearing.

Good conversationalists take the time and effort to educate themselves on topics other than business. They don't focus attention on themselves but are interested in what others have to say. They respect others' opinions and don't discount or belittle them. Good conversationalists have a good sense of humor and can laugh at themselves or bring a smile to another's face. They are welcome at any function and are enjoyed by the company they keep.

EXERCISE

List in the space below the subjects you feel most and least qualified to talk about. Then, if you can, take the opportunity to have yourself videotaped during a conversation, or have a friend or relative observe you during conversation. This will truly enlighten you about your conversational behavior. Do you interrupt when someone else is talking? Do you monopolize the conversation? Do you avoid eye contact? What is your body language saying? Review the chapter after you've been taped and jot down your assets and liabilities in conversation. Determine the behaviors that you want to correct and the others you want to continue. Each week, work on one liability until you've finished your list. Use the space below for your analysis.

Subjects Qualified to Talk About | Subjects Not Qualified to Talk About

1. _____ 1. _____
2. _____ 2. _____
3. _____ 3. _____
4. _____ 4. _____
5. _____ 5. _____

EXERCISE

Subjects Qualified to Talk About

6. ....
7. ....
8. ....
9. ....
10. ....

Subjects Not Qualified to Talk About

6. ....
7. ....
8. ....
9. ....
10. ....

Conversational Assets

1. ....
2. ....
3. ....
4. ....
5. ....
6. ....
7. ....
8. ....
9. ....
10. ....

Conversational Liabilities

1. ....
2. ....
3. ....
4. ....
5. ....
6. ....
7. ....
8. ....
9. ....
10. ....

TWENTY-TWO

Tipping

Tipping is more common in the United States than in Europe and elsewhere, where the tip is generally part of the bill. If it is not part of the bill, you are expected to tip only about 10 percent of the total bill, not the 15 percent that is customary here.

Nowadays, it seems waiters, bellmen, and taxi drivers all expect tips even when the service rendered was inadequate. For some employees, like restaurant staff, hourly wages are purposely reduced—with the balance to be made up in tips.

The word "tip" was originally an acronym for "To Insure Promptness," but somehow or another tips have become the rule regardless of the quality of service.

If you receive poor service at a restaurant, should you tip? Some feel tipping is mandatory in such cases; others disagree. Those in the first camp point out that tips represent part of the waiter's salary, and that instead of infringing on his or her income it would be better simply not to return. Those in the second camp argue that not tipping, or reducing the tip sends an immediate signal to the person regarding his or her level of service. In any case, whether you choose to tip or not, follow up your experience with a letter to the owner regarding the service received and the quality of the food ordered. Let him or her know specifically what happened so that whatever went wrong can be corrected.

In restaurants today, different services call for different tips. In most you should tip 15 percent of the total bill, but in luxury or five-star restaurants the customary tip is 20 percent. Why? Because in first class restaurants you will find at your table not only a waiter but also the captain, the busboy, and, in some cases, the wine steward, all of whom must share that 20 percent tip. In such restaurants the captain will generally get 5 percent and the waiter the remaining 15 percent. (If this is not the case, you may want to tip the captain five percent of the bill as you exit.) The busboy is not tipped by the customer directly but receives his tip from the waiter or captain.

Other rules to remember about restaurant tipping are as follows:

- When dining at a restaurant that features a buffet, the tip for the person who brings your beverages is only 10 percent, since you are basically serving yourself.
- If you are having a party of eight or more, a 15 percent gratuity will usually be added to the check automatically. If unsure whether the tip will be included, ask the restaurant manager ahead of time.
- If you want to be remembered when you return to a particular restaurant, or if you are a regular, you may want to tip the maître d' five dollars or more, depending on whether it's a modestly priced or expensive restaurant. Do this when you leave.
- The tip in hotel restaurants varies from 15 to 20 percent, depending on whether it is a modestly priced or an expensive restaurant.
- If the bill is brought on a tray, the tip should be left on the tray.
- If you use a credit card to pay, you have the option of tipping 15 percent of the total bill including tax or 15 percent of the total excluding tax. If you prefer, you may choose to leave a cash tip on the table rather than putting it on your credit card.

Many restaurants offer valet service; again, the tipping varies for each type. In cases where there is a charge for the service, tipping is, of course, not necessary. If you use the valet service at a fine restaurant, tip the parking attendant two dollars; at a modestly priced restaurant the tip is a dollar.

Many restaurants and clubs have washroom attendants. In fine establishments, the tip is one dollar per guest; at modestly priced restaurants and clubs, tip the attendant 50 cents. Note, however that you need not tip if they have not provided any service. In other words, if you get your own towel, you need not tip; if the attendant does hand you a towel, you should tip.

At restaurants, clubs, symphony halls, theaters, and other fine establishments, there will be a coat check. In many places this service is free; in others there is a small charge. At a modestly priced restaurant, the theater, symphony hall, or a casual club, tip the coatroom attendant from 25 to 75 cents per coat. At an exclusive club, country club, yacht club, or luxury restaurant, tip the attendant a dollar for each coat. Thus, if the coat charge is 75 cents for each coat, tip the attendant 25 cents. If there is no charge for this service, tip a dollar for one coat and 50 cents each for more than one.

Many restaurants have strolling musicians. If you make a musical request and the musician plays it at your table, tip him a dollar. If you have a large party of guests and they make a request that is played at the table, the tip might be about five dollars. If you are at a club and you make a request to the band or piano player, the tip should range from one to two dollars.

What about hotels, motels, planes, and trains? Hotels usually have doormen and bellmen. If the doorman takes your bags out of the car, tip him between 50 cents to a dollar. If he calls you a cab, the tip is 25 to 50 cents. According to Emily Post, the tip for the bellman varies depending on the size of the city you're visiting. In a large city, the bellman takes your bags, shows you to your room, and opens the door for you; tip him a dollar per bag and 50 cents for opening the room. In a small city, tip him 50 cents for each bag and between 50 cents and a dollar for opening the door. If you get to your room and open the door before the bellman does, tip him only for the bags.

When you order room service at a hotel, the gratuity will sometimes be added on automatically. However, this is not done in most cases. If you are unsure, check the room service menu or inquire when you call and place your order. Although there is an additional charge for room service you should still tip the room waiter 15 percent of the total bill.

Hotel maids are also tipped if they have provided good service. The tip should be about a dollar per day, to be given at the end of your stay. In first-class hotels where services were exemplary, tip the maid between five and ten dollars a week per person. In modestly priced hotels, between three and five dollars a week per person is appropriate. Tip the maid in person or leave the tip in the room when you depart. However, if you're staying at a hotel for only a day or two it's not necessary to tip.

You need not tip the valet for pressing or cleaning either, because the service charge is added to your hotel bill. Furthermore, tipping the desk clerk is not recommended unless you've stayed at the hotel over a prolonged period of time or the clerk has been especially attentive to your needs.

Other service personnel of the hotel, such as the barber, beautician, masseuse, and manicurist, are tipped the same as they are outside a hotel. Tip the barber 50 cents to a dollar for a haircut, $1 to $2 for a shampoo, shave, manicure, and cut. Tip 25 to 50 cents for children's cuts. If the hairdresser shampoos, cuts, and styles your hair, tip him or her 15 percent of the bill. If one hairdresser shampoos and another cuts, tip 20 percent of the bill; the tip will be divided evenly between the two. For facials, manicures, and pedicures, the appropriate tip is 15 percent of the total bill. Give a modest gift at Christmas to each of these people if you have been a regular customer.

Tip the masseur/masseuse between 15 to 20 percent of the bill, depending on the level of service rendered. Tip the person who shines your shoes 50 cents for a pair of shoes and a dollar for a pair of boots.

At a health or golf club, no tip is necessary unless the locker room attendant, washroom attendant, or head waiter has been especially helpful. Tip such a person $5 to $10. Golf caddies are tipped 15 percent for 18 holes and up to 20 percent for nine holes. In private clubs, like country and yacht clubs, members give to a Christmas fund, which is apportioned to employees at the holidays.

When you take a taxi, tip the driver 15 percent of the total fare. If he or she gives you above-average service, such as putting your bags in the trunk, taking them out, providing a comfortable ride, or waiting while you run an errand, tip 20 percent of the total fare. When riding in a limousine, tip the driver 15 to 20 percent of the fare.

When you fly or ride a train, you will often use the services of a skycap or porter to handle your bags. For these services, tip 50 cents to two dollars for each bag. When traveling by train, the dining car waiter receives a tip of 15 percent of the total bill. On airplanes, however, no tip is given except on a prolonged flight or if the flight attendants have been especially attentive to your needs.

Newspaper carriers, letter carriers, and other people who serve you on a regular basis are not tipped each time; however, a modest gift, either money or a small article, is given at Christmas. If you choose to give money at Christmas 5 to 15 dollars is adequate.

If you live in an apartment complex or condominium, you will want to give a small bonus at Christmas for good service. For example, give the superintendent $25 to $40, the handyman $10 to $20, the doorman $20 to $30, and the elevator operator $10.

Household employees should be tipped $5 to $10 if extra work is performed. If you stay with an associate whose maid cleans your room, tip the maid $3 to $5 for a weekend visit. Do not tip the servants if you are invited to a private party at someone's home. If you hire a maid to come once or twice a week, give her a week's pay as a bonus at Christmas time.

If you plan to travel abroad, check with your travel agent or local embassy about customary tipping practices. The percent of the total bill for tips varies from country to country, as do customs for whom and where you tip. For example, theater ushers are tipped on the continent but not in England. Find out what is customary before you go.

If someone has provided exemplary service, it's quite appropriate to give a tip of more than 15 percent of the total bill. The top level, however, is generally 20 percent of the total bill. If you become known for overtipping at a place you visit frequently, the waiters will fight over who serves you, presenting a problem for the owner or manager. Only overtip if it is well deserved, and not more than 20 percent of the total bill.

Giving a tip of less than 15 percent in a restaurant should only be done if the service is poor. If it is merely average, you should still tip 15 percent. If the food is bad but the service good, give the full 15 percent. The tip is going to the person who served your food, not to the cook. If you frequent a restaurant often and repeatedly undertip, don't expect to get any service—you will be known by the help as cheap. If you have resolved not to tip at all, then eat at home or go to a cafeteria.

If you are dining with someone who undertips, you may want to give the waiter a little extra—discreetly, without letting your host know of your action.

TWENTY-THREE

Table Manners
and Place Settings

Unlike our parents and grandparents, most of us today grew up in a world where instruction regarding appropriate table manners ranged from relaxed to virtually nonexistent. Many young adults, raised on fast food, have become experts in the art of eating with their fingers. No matter what your lifestyle, however, knowing proper table manners will come in handy when you have to be "on" during a luncheon interview, a company picnic, a business breakfast, or a cocktail buffet. Making the best impression in these situations includes not only how you look but how you manage yourself at the dining table.

I'm not suggesting that you always have to practice proper table manners; only that you should always know how. When you don't know, most of your energy and thoughts are devoted to "What is the right fork?" rather than the business at hand. Knowing the right behavior at home, in a ballroom, or at a restaurant becomes reflected in your subtle air of confidence. In other words, when you have to turn it "on," you can!

There are no exceptions regarding age, sex, religion, or race when it comes to table manners. Everyone should possess the skills to conduct him or herself properly when eating. A lot of deals are made over meals, so don't spoil your chances by fumbling around with your utensils. What kind of impression are you making when you're at a company function and you're scared stiff because you've never seen so much dinnerware on a table before? Polished executives are confident and comfortable in any of these situations because they know the ground rules.

Let's cover the basics first.

- Don't talk with your mouth full or chew with your mouth open. These are probably the two most important rules of table manners. Not only are talking with your mouth full and chewing with your mouth open unpleasant to look at, they also create unappetizing noise. Don't smack!
- Sit at the table in a comfortably erect posture. You don't need to look as though you just graduated from a military academy; however, sit comfortably straight. Don't slump.
- Have your hand in your lap while eating. Elbows on the table are inappropriate, unless you are leaning over to listen more attentively to someone. The rules on this have relaxed somewhat, to the point where you can now rest your hand and wrist on the table when eating if you'd rather not keep your hands in your lap.
- Place your napkin in your lap when you sit down. Do not tuck it into your shirt. If you are at a formal dinner, wait for your host to put his in his lap. Use your napkin to blot or pat your lips clean of food particles: avoid wiping your mouth as if it were a countertop. If you must leave the table during your meal, fold the napkin and place it on your chair and push the chair in. When you finish your meal and are leaving the table, place your napkin next to your plate on the left side. If the plates have been removed, place the napkin in the center. Don't ball up or refold it, but if there are napkin rings, put it back through the ring.
- Do not stack your dishes, either while you are eating or when you have finished.
- At a small dinner party, wait until the host begins eating before you do. At a large dinner party where there are several tables of eight or ten people, wait until your whole table is served before starting.
- Don't reach across the table to get the salt, pepper, or what have you. Ask the person closest to the item to pass it to you: "David, would you please pass the sweetener."

- When you have finished eating, place your fork, knife and other utensils used at the clock position of ten minutes to four, with the base of the utensils at the four and the sharp ends pointing to the ten.

- If you are at a private dinner party and you are served something you are allergic to, you may refuse it. Be polite when doing this, saying something like, "No, thank you." Otherwise, take a little of everything served. Nowadays it is not required or demanded that you eat everything on your plate. When declining a dish served by a waiter or waitress, just say, "No, thank you."

- The number of utensils provided depends, of course, on the number of courses to be served. The small fork on the outside left is usually for the salad. The larger, inside fork is for the entree. The knife is placed next to the plate on the right side, followed by either a teaspoon or a soup spoon, depending on what is served. The dessert fork and/or spoon is placed above the plate in the center. If both a fork and spoon are provided in this position, the fork is for the dessert and the spoon for your coffee. At any rate, the basic rule is that you start with the utensils farthest from your plate and work your way in. Sometimes you will have a shell fork at the far right, next to the spoons. This is for the appetizer, which may be escargot, clams, oysters, mussels, or other shellfish.

- When eating, there are two ways to hold your utensils: American style and European style. With the European style the primary difference is that you don't move the fork to your other hand once you've cut your meat. Instead you bring the food to your mouth with your left hand. The American style, however, is probably preferable. When in Rome, do as the Romans do.

   With the American style you hold the fork in your right hand when bringing the food to your mouth. When you are cutting your food, put the fork in your left hand and the knife in your right, cut the food (one to three pieces at a time), place the knife horizontally at the top of your plate, and switch the fork (with the food still on it) to your right hand before bringing it toward your mouth. The fork should rest across your middle finger with your index finger and thumb over the top. When cutting your food, place the fork, with the prongs facing downward, between the middle and index fingers, with the index finger straight and resting on the back of the fork and the thumb bracing it from underneath. The knife should be held in the right hand in a similar fashion. (Of course, lefthanders will want to reverse the process just described.)

■ When presented with a finger bowl at the end of the meal, don't dip your napkin in the bowl and wipe off your mouth. The finger bowl is for your fingers only. If you are presented with a warm damp cloth, the same rule applies. Fingers only.

■ Don't use your fingers to push food onto your fork; if necessary, use a cracker or a small piece of bread.

■ With soup, use the larger, round spoon rather than the teaspoon. Draw the soup away from you, rather than toward you. Do not pick up the bowl to catch the last drops; tilt the bowl away from you with one hand and spoon the remaining soup. Don't slurp. If the soup bowl has a plate underneath, place the spoon on this plate; otherwise, place the spoon in the soup bowl.

■ When serving yourself butter, put the amount you will need on your butter or salad plate. Do not hold up the passing by taking the butter directly from the dish and buttering your bread. With potatoes, the same rule applies: take a pat of butter and put it on your butter plate or directly on your potato. Gravies and salad dressings should be put directly on the food items when served.

■ The butter knife, when not in use, should be placed diagonally or horizontally at the top of the bread plate. Break the bread into three or four pieces before buttering and eating.

■ If you take a mouthful of food that is too hot, quickly take a swallow of water. If no beverage is available, spit the food discreetly onto your fork. Do this with spoiled food as well. Place the food, in either case, on the edge of your dinner plate.

■ If you have to sneeze or blow your nose, cover your nose and your mouth with a tissue or handkerchief. If you don't have either, or the time, use your napkin or your hand. Don't use the napkin to blow your nose. If your sneezing continues over a prolonged period, excuse yourself to the restroom.

- If you are at a private home and you discover an unwelcome addition to your food, such as a bug or a hair, don't call attention to it. Simply take the item and place it discreetly at the edge of your plate. If disgust prevents you from continuing your meal, stop eating. At a restaurant, quietly call the waiter's attention to the problem and ask for a replacement.

- Toothpicks should not be used at the table; wait until you leave. If you are bothered by food stuck between your teeth, excuse yourself to the restroom and remove it. Whatever you do, don't pick the food out with your fingers.

- Don't wash your food down with a liquid. Chew and swallow before you take a drink.

- Don't try to wipe the tableware clean. If you get a dirty fork at a restaurant, call your waiter's attention to it in a discreet manner and ask for a replacement. If you are given only one fork for several courses at a restaurant, you may ask for a replacement with each course or lay the used fork on your salad or bread plate.

- Don't use your utensils as props when speaking at the table. If you have a tendency to talk with your hands, lay your utensils down. Of course, gesturing with utensils bearing food is out of the question.

- Don't take huge amounts of food into your mouth.

- Salad may be cut into smaller pieces with the knife while you are eating it. Do not, however, cut it all up and toss it before you begin.

- Women, don't freshen up your lipstick before a meal. Lipstick stains on a glass are not a pretty sight. If you are at a private dinner party at someone's home, you won't want to ruin their napkins with your lipstick.

- Whether you are at a home or in a restaurant, your handbag should never be left on the table.

- Unless you're eating a hamburger or something equally folksy, don't ask for catsup. It's an insult to the cook and to the rest of your party, including your host.

- If, at a restaurant, you have to spend time on the telephone, don't bring the phone to your table; go to the public telephones outside the restrooms. Better yet, abstain from doing business when you are with guests. Be as discreet as possible when you have to take a phone call by excusing yourself from the table and returning quietly.

- Do not "table hop" at a restaurant or large party. It's rude.
- Do not fix your hair at the table.
- If you must burp, do so discreetly and cover your mouth.
- When hosting a party of ten or more at a restaurant, preorder the meal.
- Keep the noise down. Being loud at a restaurant is annoying to other customers.
- If you want to taste someone else's food, or if he wants to try yours, don't lean over to each other's plates and take what you want. Hand your fork over and let him get a piece for you—or, before you start eating, put a little on the edge of his plate.
- At a restaurant, don't order more courses than others in your party. For example, if everyone orders an entree, don't order an appetizer. It only slows up the meal.
- Don't drink your meal. Calling for a second drink before the meal arrives is unacceptable. Whether you're a man or a woman, being tipsy or drunk is ugly.
- When food is served family style, it is polite to hold the dish while the person next to you serves herself. When you pass, pass to the right, whether a woman or a man is seated there.
- When you have finished eating, don't push back your plate or lean back and say, "I'm done!"
- If you must complain about something, do it discreetly. Once you have tried with the waiter and the head waiter and nothing was done, approach the manager. You may corner the manager away from other guests and tell him or her about the matter that bothered you. Follow it up with a letter, also to the manager. (If the service was excellent, let the manager know that, too, and be specific.)
- If no one at your table is smoking, then don't smoke. Nowadays there are smoking and nonsmoking sections in restaurants. If you're in the nonsmoking section, don't smoke. If you are seated in the smoking section, ask whether anyone minds before you light up. If you are at someone's home and you don't see any ashtrays, take it as a signal

that the host doesn't want you to smoke. Don't smoke in the bathroom! Do not smoke cigars.

Smoking. In earlier years, the perception of smoking was relatively positive. Movies often showed "lighting up" as a means of socialization, especially between men and women. However, smoking is perceived very differently in American society today. Contemporary films are more likely to portray smokers as people with severe stress or psychological problems who must smoke to cope with the world around them. The dangers to nonsmokers of second-hand smoke have also been widely discussed.

This means that, if you are a smoker, you have a strike against you when you smoke in public or in a professional setting. I'm not going to tell you to quit smoking; I will tell you, however, that the perceptions others will have of you as a smoker are going to be strongly negative. Today, smoking is associated with cancer, emphysema, and early death. If you choose to smoke, remember that your identification as a smoker can have a profound undermining effect on your efforts to build a positive image.

Remember that a cigarette hanging loosely from the mouth is not a pretty sight. Don't leave your cigarette unattended in an ashtray; always hold on to it. When inhaling, you should put the cigarette in your mouth toward the left or right side, rather than in the center. When exhaling, you should blow the smoke either up or down—not into someone's face. Tap your cigarette lightly once on the ashtray to dispose of ashes. Do not chain smoke around others, even other smokers.

If you are setting the table for a multi-course meal, begin from the left with the napkin, salad fork, dinner fork, dinner plate, dinner knife with the blade turned inward, soup spoon, and teaspoon. The bread and butter plate is placed on the upper left-hand side, with the butter knife laid directly across it in a diagonal direction. At the upper right-hand side, in direct line with your knife, are the glasses; first the water glass, then the wine glass(es), then the champagne and sherry glasses. The champagne and sherry glasses can also be placed in front the water and wine glass(es) so that all glasses are seen. The dessert fork or spoon is placed either above the plate in the center with the handle on the right or on the left between the dinner plate and the dinner fork. If you choose, you can put the napkin in the middle of the plate, folded, rather than on the left side. The coffee cup, saucer, and spoon are placed to the right of the glasses.

EXERCISE

Go to the china department of a department store or to a china specialty store. Observe the table settings and determine how many courses they are set up for. Practice table setting at home for a single-course meal (the entree), a two-course meal (salad and entree), and a three-course meal (salad, entree, and dessert). Next, review the tips for appropriate behavior and incorporate them when dining.

TWENTY-FOUR

When You're the Host

Have you ever been at a party that you remembered for years to come? The music was perfect, the guests were exciting, and the food was out of this world. Or perhaps you were invited to lunch or dinner, and everything went so smoothly you didn't realize how quickly time flew. It's amazing what a difference it makes when an event is hosted by someone who really knows how.

Part of projecting the executive image is the ability to entertain clients and business associates with flair. Business entertaining is a major component of an executive's job description. The reasons to entertain are several: returning someone else's generous hospitality, thanking a client for business, making contact with a new person. Perhaps it's your boss's birthday or your partner's. Maybe you want to honor an institution or person who has served the community well. There is just one rule to bear in mind: if you are returning someone's hospitality, keep your event in line with what that person did. For example, if Mr. and Mrs. Jones took you to a fancy restaurant, buying them cocktails will not repay them; you'll need to host a dinner at a nice restaurant or invite them to the opera.

Whether the party is for two or five hundred, the host has many responsibilities that must be attended to in order for the event to be successful. He or she must decide where to hold the event, what to serve, and what kind of music to have; the guest list must be drawn up and the invitations must be sent. The list of details can seem endless.

What does it take to be a good host? Let's identify the host's responsibilities in different environments. After all, when you invite someone to lunch or dinner at a restaurant, you are the host. When you have a dinner party at your home, club, or restaurant, you are the host. When you invite a client or associate to a baseball game or other sporting event, you are the host. And when you invite someone to the theater, opera, or symphony, you are the host. Here are some guidelines to keep in mind in these situations.

When you are returning someone's generosity and your budget won't allow the same expense lavished on you, you should certainly invite the person to a modest restaurant and a movie or a fine meal served at your home. Remember that your options for entertaining go beyond evening events such as dinner, cocktails, and the theater: why not consider breakfast or tea, lunch at your office or home, or lunch at a restaurant, or a family-oriented activity such as ice skating or swimming? Your options as host are as endless as your creativity will allow. Whatever you choose to do, however, give it all you've got and make it special.

For example, when you invite someone over for dinner, give them a good meal—not pizza or fast food hamburgers. If you invite someone to lunch at your home or office, put out nice plates, napkins, and utensils as well as something worthwhile to eat. If you're not much of a cook, have the event catered, buy some pre-made entrees at a gourmet deli, or take your guests to a restaurant.

When it comes to restaurant dining, there are several guidelines to make the event comfortable for everyone invited. First, pick a restaurant you've been to before. If you don't know what your guest's likes or dislikes are when it comes to food, pick a place that serves a variety of fish, fowl, and beef.

The host pays in all situations. Nowadays it's common for a woman to invite a male client to dinner. Women, if you feel there might be tension when the check arrives, settle the issue before you sit down. Taking care of the check with a credit card in advance is a lot easier for some men to handle—and a much more polished approach than fumbling around with money when the check arrives.

When you make your restaurant reservations, check which credit cards are accepted and ask about the dress code. Make your reservations in advance, especially if you are hosting a party of six or more and the restaurant is a popular one. It is embarrassing to wait twenty minutes for your name to be called for a table. Furthermore, if you have to cancel the reservation, or if the number in your party changes, notify the restaurant.

As the host you select the time and the date. Know your plans when you call to extend the invitation. If your guest cannot attend that day, have an alternate date ready. Be sure to do the inviting at least three to seven days in advance. If it's a special client, an old friend, or a large party, extend the invitation two weeks in advance. Never invite someone at the last minute.

Once a guest has accepted your invitation, don't change the date unless it's an absolute emergency. If this happens, call the person yourself. Don't leave a message with her secretary at work or on her answering machine at home—it will look as though you're avoiding her. If you must cancel, propose another time in the near future when you can get together. When the date is set, call the day before, if it's a breakfast meeting, or first thing in the morning, if it's luncheon or dinner. This is particularly important if you have to drive any distance to get to the restaurant or if you have to pick your guest up.

At the Restaurant

If you are arriving in separate cars, make sure you arrive on time, if not a few minutes early. This will allow you to settle the check in advance and greet your guest or guests when she/they arrive. As the host, you are best advised to wait in the entry of the restaurant rather than at the table—unless the restaurant does not take reservations and you notice that the place is filling up. In that case, take your seat at a table. Some restaurants will not seat a party until all are present. Check this out beforehand.

When everyone is assembled, the restaurant personnel will escort you to your table. Follow your guests to the table so that they can be seated first. In the case of a large party, have in mind who will sit next to whom. If there's a guest of honor, that person should sit at the head of the table, while the host sits at the other end—assuming yours is a rectangular table. If it's a round table, the guest of honor will sit to the right of the host.

Suppose your guest is late—how long should you wait? If you've been waiting at least fifteen minutes, call his office to ask after his whereabouts. If your guest is fortunate enough to own a car phone, you may want to try that number to see if he is on his way. Go to the table, order a drink, and wait forty minutes. If he still hasn't shown up, either order a meal or give the waiter a five to ten-dollar tip. Why? Because you have kept a table for a period of time when there could have been paying customers.

When you invite people to a restaurant you're familiar with, make suggestions about good selections. If the restaurant has a reputation for a particular item, mention it. Budget allowing, suggest that your guests order appetizers. Remember, guests order first; you order last. If someone at your table orders an expensive dish, then order one as well. If everyone has ordered an appetizer, you should order one too.

When the food arrives, wait until everyone is served before beginning. As the host, you give the signal for everyone to eat by picking up your own fork. The same applies to drinks, if the people at your table have ordered cocktails: the host is the first to raise a glass. With a large function, however, if the course is a hot one, advise your guests to go ahead and begin eating.

Here are some other things to consider when you invite someone to a restaurant. If there is a bad seat at the table, take it yourself. You may ask the restaurant manager for another one, but do this discreetly. If one of your guests is in a wheelchair or is large, make sure that person sits in a location where he does not trouble anyone if he has to excuse himself. And if one of your guests eats slowly, you can ask, when everyone else has finished, whether she minds if the waiter brings the next course.

Hosting a function someplace other than a restaurant calls for additional planning. First, you'll want to define what kind of function it is—a dinner party, a cocktail party, a buffet or a reception. If it's a dinner party, you'll want to determine what the occasion is—say, a birthday or a promotion. That will determine how many people are invited, and when and where the party is held.

The main ingredients for a successful dinner party are congenial guests, a well-planned menu, an attractive table, well-prepared food, and good help. Most of the work should be done in advance so that when the evening event arrives, you can be your cordial self. The degree of formality of all these components is up to you, but each of them is crucial to the success of any function.

Dinner Parties

Invitations to a dinner party should be sent out two to three weeks in advance. The invitation should state the occasion to be celebrated, the date, the time, the type of dress, the name of the host, and the location. If the location of the party is difficult to find, include a map. The invitation should close with "R.S.V.P." (translation: "please respond") followed by your phone number. If you want, you may request that guests R.S.V.P. by a certain date.

When you make up your guest list, try to choose people who will be interesting to each other. Do not invite people you know don't like each other.

If you plan to serve cocktails before dinner, time the meal to be served an hour later. Otherwise, dinner should be served twenty minutes after the time indicated on the invitation. If yours is a dinner party at your home, you'll want to wait about fifteen minutes before serving dinner.

When dinner is served, the water glasses should already be filled. The placement of guests should be decided in advance, and, depending on the formality of the occasion, placecards may be created to identify where people should sit. You'll want to have a girl-boy-girl-boy arrangement, with the guest of honor at one end and you at the other, or the honored guest seated to the right of you.

If you decide to use hired help for the occasion, call around to different catering services before selecting one. Meet with them several times to discuss plans and arrangements. If you plan on cooking the food at home and hire a maid and a bartender to help, they should arrive several hours before the event begins.

Depending on the level of formality, you may want several courses or just one. Once dinner is over, coffee is served. Consider making a pot each of regular and decaffeinated, since many people today avoid caffeine, particularly in the evening. You may choose to serve the coffee in another room along with a selection of liqueurs.

Receptions

A reception is often held in honor of a public or prominent figure or event, or when parents want to give a party for their newly married son or daughter.

The difference between a reception and a cocktail party are very slight. Technically, no liquor is served at a reception, but this rule is seldom observed. A reception is almost never given for women only, and there is always a receiving line. Receptions run for about two hours, in late afternoon—say four to six—early evening—say five to seven—or late evening—say ten to twelve. (A late evening reception is usually timed to follow a performance and attended by the principal performers.) Guests at a reception have the choice of punch or a drink at a bar. Finger foods, such as sandwiches, mints, nuts, meatballs, cheese and crackers, and olives are often served. The food is not meant to take the place of a meal but to serve as an appetizer. Be sure to have cocktail napkins available for drinks and food.

Receptions are relatively formal affairs; dress should be coat and tie. Background music should be soft enough that people can hear one another in conversation but loud enough to fill in any voids.

Cocktail Parties

Cocktail parties are great for repaying friends and acquaintances who have invited you to lots of parties. They are also an opportunity to entertain new acquaintances and business associates. A cocktail party, like a reception, is usually held for a set period of time, most often late afternoon from four to six or from five to seven. R.S.V.P.'s are usually omitted from the invitation. Hors d'oeuvres and appetizers are served in modest quantities. Small paper napkins should be provided with cocktails, and larger napkins, either paper or cloth, should be provided with the hors d'oeuvres.

When determining what drinks to stock and in what quantity, estimate that each guest will have at least three drinks. Stock up on vodka, gin, vermouth, whiskey, scotch, wines, and beer, as well as cool water and both diet and regular soft drinks. You should also have on hand green olives, orange slices, maraschino cherries, limes, and lemons. Your selection of glasses should include tall and short ten-ounce sizes, as well as wine glasses.

A note about alcohol. The law in many states makes the party-giver liable for alcohol-related driving accidents, so be prepared to call a taxi for someone who seems even slightly tipsy. Take away his or her keys and ask a friend to drive, or, if it's someone you know well, ask the person to stay the night. You'll really be doing him a favor.

Cocktail Buffets

The difference between a cocktail party and a cocktail buffet is that in the case of the latter the amount and type of food served is enough to make a meal. The invitation will state the time of arrival but not that of departure, in order to give the guests more time to mingle and eat. The invitation will also have an R.S.V.P. with the phone number so that enough food is prepared.

Be prepared to serve your guests well. You could have little sandwiches of thinly sliced beef, chicken, or ham with mustard and mayonnaise. You might consider chicken wings, dips, tacos, cheese fondue, or steak tartar for a substantial buffet. Remember, it's better to have too much than too little. If you are limited on time, grocery stores and caterers provide an ample selection of food trays to satisfy the pickiest gourmet.

The table should be covered by a tablecloth and equipped with small cocktail plates, utensils, napkins, and food. Brighten it with a centerpiece of flowers or appropriate decorations for a holiday festivity. For a Christmas cocktail buffet, for example, you could consider a centerpiece of Christmas balls, pine cones, red ribbon, and pine ferns. Dress for cocktails or cocktail buffets will vary depending on the formality of the occasion.

EXERCISE 1

Reread the guidelines for hosting an event at a restaurant, then invite a friend or business associate to lunch, incorporating these guidelines.

EXERCISE 2

Create a mock dinner party, cocktail party, reception, or cocktail buffet. Using the guidelines mentioned in this chapter, create a mock invitation, guest list, menu, music/atmosphere, time, occasion, and table setting.

EXERCISE

TWENTY-FIVE

When You're the Guest

Polite guests reward the time and effort of throwing a party, and they are remembered for this. Indeed, an essential part of projecting the executive image is conducting yourself properly when invited to a restaurant, a reception, or the company picnic. As your client's or boss's guest, you are being evaluated in these environments. Being a good guest contributes to your success.

There is no question that guest manners in our society are deteriorating. Thank-you notes are virtually unheard of. Guests arrive late and provide little help in the kitchen. Granted, societal trends may account for more casual atmospheres when it comes to entertaining; yet this cannot excuse plain bad manners. Guests have responsibilities too, for the success of any party depends on them.

Following are some hints on how to be a dream guest.

Restaurants

■ When you are invited to lunch or dinner, remember that it is not your responsibility to pick up the check. In this case I'm speaking more to men than women. Nowadays it is common for a woman to invite a professional colleague to lunch. If it truly is an invitation, let her pick up the check.

- When a client, associate, or your boss invites you to dinner, give your response within twenty-four hours. If you are still not sure by then for legitimate reasons, ask whether you can reschedule for a time when you know you can attend. If you don't care to meet with the person, just say "Thank you, but I can't make it on the twentieth," or "I'm busy on the twentieth." If you can't go that day but want to get together, suggest another day in the immediate future.

- If something comes up and you have to cancel, place the call yourself. Don't have your secretary or anyone else call for you, and don't leave a message on an answering machine. Remember, you should only cancel a date because of a dire emergency. Getting another offer for that night is not a dire emergency. Perhaps the second offer can be rescheduled.

- Confirm an appointment, whether it's for breakfast, lunch, or dinner. If it's for breakfast, call the day before and confirm, if the host hasn't already called. Call the same day to confirm luncheon and dinner appointments.

- It is important, whether you've been invited to a restaurant, home, or ballroom, that you arrive on time. Ten minutes late is considered rude. If you know you're going to be late, call to change the time, if possible, or call the restaurant to have your host notified. If you arrive so late that your host and the other guests are already seated, order something quickly. If they are eating the first course, order a first course. Order whatever course they are currently eating, even if it's dessert. Apologize to your host for your tardiness.

- If you happen to beat your host to the restaurant, wait in the lobby or entry hall until she arrives. If you notice that the restaurant is filling up quickly, you can ask the restaurant host to seat you and to have the rest of the party directed there as they arrive. When you are seated at the table, don't start eating the bread or crackers or order a drink immediately. Wait a while; when your host is fifteen minutes late, you may order a drink. You want the table to look untouched.

- If your host is at least fifteen minutes overdue, call his or her office. Perhaps a road accident has held up traffic. Wait for your host for about forty minutes. If she still hasn't shown up, either tip the waiter five to ten dollars or have something to eat.

- When there are more than two people in the party, don't sit down immediately when you've been led to your table: wait for the host to direct you. That may be the guest of honor's seat!

- When in a large party, observe what other people are ordering. If they haven't ordered an appetizer or salad, don't be the only one. And don't order the most expensive item on the menu simply because it's the most expensive. If there are other selections you would enjoy just as much, order those instead. Your host will appreciate the gesture. However, if your host urges you to order whatever you want, including the most expensive item, you may order it.

- When there are just two of you at a restaurant, it's polite to wait until both have been served before eating. If there is a long delay, then the one who has not been served should urge the other to start eating while the food is hot. Of course, if it's a cold entree, like a salad, there is no need to start eating before your companion has been served.

    In larger parties, when a guest of honor is not present, the host will wait until everyone is served before beginning. If the table has a guest of honor, that person must wait for everyone to be served. If it's a large party and the food is hot, the guest of honor should begin when he or she is served.

- At a dinner where spouses or partners are present, remember to talk about other subjects than business.

- If someone tells a good joke or you're having a great time, it's okay to laugh; just keep the noise level down so that it doesn't interfere with others.

- Don't "table hop."

- If you must make or receive a telephone call, excuse yourself and go to a phone away from the table. Keep your conversation short.

When you receive an invitation for dinner or cocktails, you should reply as soon as possible. Even if there isn't an R.S.V.P. on the invitation, a polite guest calls the host to let him know whether she can come. Some invitations will have a specific date to reply by. Be polite and reply by the time allocated. Otherwise, you could mess up your host's plans for food and table set-up.

Even if it's your best buddy giving an informal potluck supper, it's only polite that you let your friend know whether you will be there and what you can bring.

- Guests should arrive to a dinner at the time specified on the invitation. If you are more than fifteen minutes late, you should approach your host (even if he has sat down to eat) and apologize. The host will probably serve you the course that they are on.
- For a cocktail party scheduled for 5:00 P.M. to 7:00 P.M., you should arrive no later than 5:30 and leave no earlier than 6:30.
- A polite guest doesn't overstay his or her welcome. If you arrived late, it doesn't mean that you can stay late. Don't be the last to leave. And please don't wait for the host to say, "Let's call it a night."
- If you're at a dinner party and the host offers you something you can't eat or drink, simply say, "No, thank you." Don't give your host the whole tale about being allergic to the food or following a special diet. Mention it to him or her when you leave the party.
- When you leave a party, say goodbye to the people you were talking to and to the host. When saying goodbye to the host(s), remember to thank them for the evening. If the party has a guest of honor, it is important to say goodbye to this person as well.
- When a single person has a party in his or her home and does not have hired help, invited guests should offer to help in the kitchen both before and after the meal. When the main course is finished, it would also be a polite gesture to help remove the dishes for the host. I think the important part is to offer the help. If the host says no, fine; however, he may find it difficult to ask for needed help, so do make the offer. Your gesture will be well taken and remembered.
- When you are invited to someone's home for a cocktail party, reception, or dinner party, it's always a welcome gesture to bring the host flowers (if she is a woman), a bottle of wine, a box of candy, or some other gift just to show your appreciation for the invitation. Refrain from elaborate gifts; these can only make your host uneasy and cause the other guests to question your relationship with the host(s).

Here are some guidelines for guests that apply to any and all situations.

- Allow yourself one drink per hour at most, and if you find yourself getting high, switch to soda. If you don't drink and you feel odd at a cocktail party, just have club soda with a lime. No one will know. As a guest, don't push drinks on anyone! If you recently underwent treatment for alcoholism or drugs, you may want to consider declining such affairs until you feel completely confident about your abstinence.

  Don't get drunk! If you have had too much to drink, however, allow someone who is sober to drive you home. Perhaps the host offers to call you a cab; take it. Don't call the attention of the other guests to this kind of assistance—doing so is more embarrassing for you than for them.

  Moreover, if you get outright drunk, don't become loud, obnoxious, or embarrassing at the party. It's time for you to "call it a night"— or regret you ever came. If you came alone, call a cab or ask a friend to drive you home.

- Do not indulge in loud arguments or discussions. In other words, don't get hostile with the other guests. If you start to become angry with someone or something at the party, either leave or get a breath of fresh air. You can just say, "Excuse me, please, I need to freshen up," or just "Excuse me, please, it's been a pleasure speaking with you, but I must tend to an important matter; thank you for the conversation."

- After any party, write a thank you note. This gesture is extremely important whether the party was a social or a business one. Even when you've thanked your host at the door, a thank-you note is sincerely appreciated and remembered. The note need not be long; in fact, the simpler the better. Either type it on company letterhead or write it by hand on a small note card in a neat, concise manner. See Chapter 26 for more details.

TWENTY-SIX

A Letter for All Occasions

When was the last time you got a thank you note? Seems that gesture no longer exists; however, that simple effort can make a world of difference in boosting your professional career. I frequently write thank you notes. Whether it is to thank someone for a gift, a good luncheon meeting (where they picked up the tab) or just the pleasure of meeting someone—I send a note. Whether it's for a present, dinner, or a weekend stay, a thank you note is essential and it makes a big difference. I once was introduced to someone at a professional function and he said, "Yes I remember you, you sent me that lovely thank you note (no kidding!)."

Some of us were never taught the importance of a thank you note or other forms of written communication such as letters in establishing and maintaining our professional network, but letter writing is critical in business and promoting your image and career. For example, after a job interview a thank you note to the interviewer gives you another opportunity to remind them of your interview and further explain questions that were asked during it. If you flubbed up on a question during your interview, the thank you note is an opportunity for reprieve.

This chapter will provide guidelines for all types of written correspondence including the thank you note, and letters of application and condolences. Further, stationary issues and letter format, such as salutations and closings will be discussed as it pertains to enhancing your executive image.

Finally, examples will be provided to help you create your own written correspondence with success.

When writing letters in business, most should be typewritten for ease of reading. When it comes to a thank you note, even in business you have the option of either hand or typewritten. If your handwriting is difficult to read, you might consider typing the note instead. When you do handwrite a business thank you, strive for neatness and clarity .

Further, check spelling and accuracy of what you're saying. I'd suggest that you read it out loud since often our eyes jump over mistakes. If using a word processor with spell check, still check your spelling. Make absolutely sure that you've spelled the person's name correctly and list their correct title. If unsure call and find out. Do not send any correspondence with "Dear Sir or Madam."

Be sure that your address and the person's address are in the letter. How many times have you gotten a letter, particularly a Christmas card, without a return address anywhere on the card or envelope. Moreover, when writing any business correspondence get right to the point. Besides these tidbits, let's delve deeper into letter format.

Format

There are three types of letter formats: semi-block, modified-block and full block (Figures 1-3). With the full-block format all lines begin flush with the left margin. This includes the date (and your address if not on letterhead), the name, title, and address of the individual that you're writing to, the salutation, each paragraph of the letter, the closing, signature, and references, i.e., Enclosure. The paragraphs in the full-block format are NOT indented.

With modified block, the date (and address if not on letterhead) is centered toward the top of the page. The individual's name and address, salutation, and all paragraphs are all flush left. The closing and signature are centered while the references are also flush left. With semi-block, the only difference between this and modified block is that the paragraphs are indented five spaces.

Some specifics regarding your business correspondence: First, write your letter on white, gray, or cream paper. Avoid fluorescent, baby blue, lavender, and so forth. The color of your paper should coordinate with other materials that are included. Furthermore, your letter should be single-spaced with a double space between the paragraphs. Moreover, between the date and the individual's address should be four spaces, between the address and the salutation—two spaces, and between the salutation and the first paragraph—two spaces. Between the last sentence of the last paragraph and the closing should be two spaces while between the closing and the signature should be four. Between the signature and the references should be two.

Page numbering is needed for business correspondence that exceeds one page. Even in personal notes, include page numbers to help the reader understand the contents. The page number is usually placed in the top right corner about four inches down and in line with the right hand margin. You can also use a header and a page number to help the reader keep all pages together and in correct order.

Most business correspondence is on 8½" by 11" paper that is folded twice to form three folds that are equivalent in width. This will allow the letter to fit neatly in a size 10 envelope which is the standard business size.

Salutations: Salutations are greetings such as "Dear . . ." As mentioned earlier the salutation should include the person's name not "Dear Sir or Madam." Although the best salutation is "Dear . . ." you can also use "My very dear Dr. Seitz," however, that may be perceived as too mushy. If you know the person well you can use their first name such as "Dear Victoria." When you sign the letter make sure you write your name and below type your name. Otherwise, if writing a thank you note to someone you just met be formal as in "Dear Dr. Seitz." Further, if they have a title as I do, include that title such as "Dear Senator Graham," or "Dear Judge Seitz."

When it comes to persons without titles use either Mr., Mrs., or Ms. If you are writing to a businesswoman who is married find out how she would like to be addressed. Some prefer Mrs. as opposed to Ms. But giving her that choice will certainly make points for your image. If you don't know if a woman is married or not, then address her as Ms. The punctuation after the salutation is a colon in business correspondence (always on company letterhead) and a comma when addressing a friend in an informal letter.

When writing the letter try to avoid the pronoun "I." Particularly in a thank you note, employ the pronoun "you." For example, "Dear Ms. Smith:

Thank you so very much for taking time to share your expertise with the students. You were right on target with the information presented as demonstrated by their intense interest and questions following."

Sometimes business correspondence includes an attention line that highlights the specific content of the letter. The attention line is situated two spaces down, flush left from the inside address. An example of an attention line is "Re: January 1st column." An attention line can also be incorporated into a letter when you're unsure of the person that you're writing to as in the case of answering an ad for a job "Re: Marketing Director's Advertisement, *The Sun*, January 31st."

Closings: The closing is essentially a good-bye. Although we often don't see "Good-bye" as a closing for a letter, that is the role the closing serves. The most common closing is "Sincerely," however, there are many more available. When deciding the closing to use look at the salutation for direction. For example, if writing someone for the first time the salutation is "Dear." The suggested closing would be "Sincerely." When writing an old business friend the salutation might be "Dearest Bob," while the closing is "Very sincerely yours." As shown, when writing the closing only the first word should be capitalized such as "Very truly yours." Moreover, a comma follows the closing. Don't even consider abbreviating a closing, rather spell it out. Some other closings that you might consider include the following:

Cordially	Very truly yours
Cordially yours	Yours cordially
Respectfully	Yours respectfully
Respectfully yours	Yours sincerely
Sincerely yours	Yours truly
Truly yours	Yours very respectfully
Very cordially yours	Yours very cordially
Very respectfully yours	Yours very sincerely
Very sincerely yours	Yours very truly

Signature and Responsibility: After the closing is your signature. Depending on the nature of the letter and the level of formality you may write your first name only or your full name. This is not the time to be practicing for a superstar signature that is illegible or overly large but just sign your name. Below your signature type your full name and your title or responsibility. For example, "Victoria A. Seitz, Ph.D., Instructor." Your responsibility may be after your name or the next line below your type-written name.

References: References include notations on who typed the letter if typed by someone other than you, post scripts, notations of enclosures, or carbon copies (cc:). The reference is located two spaces below the typed signature and flush left. If noting the typist and that there are enclosures, your initials in capitals should be listed first followed by a colon followed by the typists initials in lower case. Then go one space down and type "Enclosure" if one, or "Enclosures," if more than one. If sending carbon copies note this one space down flush left with "cc:" in lower case letters along with the names of the persons who are receiving copies.

Envelopes: With all letters, social or business, include your return address. The return address should be located either in the upper left hand corner of the envelope or on the back flap. Include your name, company name, address, city, state, and zip code. Sometimes a company logo is included in addition to or in place of the company name.

The name of the person that you're writing to should be placed half way between the top or bottom of the envelope in the center. The address should be in block style and include the persons name and title, company name on the next line, followed by the address, city, state, and zip code on the following lines. An example of the format is as follows:

Dr. Jean Fairhust
University of Oklahoma
Department of Business and Public Administration
5500 University Parkway
Norman, OK 74711

or

Mr. Robert Dorney, Marketing Director
Canine Nutrition Experts
41088 Canyon Hill Road, Suite 21
Rancho Cucamonga, CA 91641

Window envelopes are for formal correspondence such as invoices and other types of correspondence sent in bulk such as form letters, i.e. "Our records show that your account has expired and we would like to know if you want to reopen it."

Memos: Memos are used to communicate internally among peers, departments, subordinates, and supervisors. Some companies provide stationary for memos or "Memorandums," but most times you have to come up with your own. Formats for memos are simple with either "Memo" or "Memorandum" centered at the top of the page followed by four spaces and then flush left:

Date:

To:

From:

Re:

Two spaces are between each line. Be sure to either sign the memo at the end of it or initial it after your name on the "FROM" line.

Stationary: Stationary used for business might include company letterhead or plain paper. Again, as mentioned previously, use white, cream, gray, or gray-blue colors and avoid baby blue, and florescent colored papers.

For thank you notes consider either purchasing fold over note cards that are tailored and say "thank you" on the front or use company letterhead. If you are handwriting the note use a fold over note card. If ordering personalized stationary for thank you notes you may want to have your initials at top or your name followed by your credentials such as "Ph.D." or "MBA" at top such as "Victoria A. Seitz, Ph.D..". Also, when writing a business note for personal use, such as writing the electric company regarding your house bill, just use white bond paper with your home address at the top. Do not use company letterhead.

Electronic Mail (E-mail)

E-mail correspondence is usually a memorandum and written in that format. The only difference between a hard copy memo and an electronic one is that, as of yet, they cannot be signed or initialed. However, even though you write the memo in the proper format, because of the different systems available your communication may not arrive in their computer in the same format. Don't worry about that but do worry that punctuation, spelling, and grammar are correct.

Samples of Different Types of Correspondence

Thank-you note: (i.e., for lunch)

Dear Mr. Martin:

Thank you so very much for a memorable lunch. You certainly know how to pick the restaurants. The food was terrific.

Also, thank you for taking time to review and comment on the product proposal. I believe that Cameo can take your company in the direction you want to go. I will call you next week to discuss a finalized proposal.

Again, thanks for a great time. I look forward to talking with you next week.

Sincerely,

Victoria Seitz, Ph.D..

Letter of Application: (i.e., for a job)

Dear Dr. Swenson:

I would like to be considered as a candidate for the assistant professor's position in the College of Home Economics. I learned of this position through Dr. Lynn Sisler, my dissertation advisor.

During my tenure at Oklahoma State I have taught a variety of subjects in the area including Fashion Design and Textiles. In addition, I have conducted joint research with faculty in the areas of direct marketing and clothing for the disabled. For example, I recently co-authored a study of Internet purchasing of clothing with Dr. Betty Gaffney which was submitted to the Journal of Home Economics. The enclosed vitae gives complete information regarding my background and experience. I believe that I can be an asset to your department given my experience in the fashion business and graduate learning.

I will call you in the next couple of weeks regarding an interview. If there are any questions or comments do not hesitate to contact me at (715) 883-9876. I look forward to talking with you.

Sincerely,

Marie S. Perkins

Letter of Application:

Dear Dr. Helder:

Dr. Norton Marks suggested that I contact you regarding the position for Marketing Director at your firm. I would like to be considered as a candidate for the position.

Enclosed is my resume that gives detailed information regarding my background and experience. I worked as a Marketing Assistant for Burdines department stores for the past five years. During this time I reorganized how advertising was conducted for the corporation and initiated an evaluation process for annual reviews of our marketing program. Further, I helped develop the new logo and slogan "What's right is here" for the chain. These, along with the other responsibilities that I handled, gave me the opportunity to help Burdines make a successful turnaround. Further, with these experiences I would be an asset to making Georgia Products the successful company that it wants to be.

I will call you in the next ten days regarding an interview. If there are any questions or comments do not hesitate to call me at (909) 889-5678. I look forward to talking with you.

Sincerely,

John Bass

Letter Acknowledging Application:

Dear Dr. Howard:

This is to acknowledge receipt of your application for the Chair of Marketing at Maybarry University.

As explained in the advertisement you answered, we plan to make a decision by May. The search committee will review the applications and proceed with interviews of the top three candidates no later than April.

Again, thank you for your interest in Maybarry University.

Sincerely,

Eldon Scribner, Ph.D., Dean
School of Business and Management

Letter of Condolence:

Dear Mrs. Robinson:

    I am so sorry to hear of the loss of J.C. He was an outstanding individual and helped me to succeed at the University. His wry sense of humor and enthusiasm for life made the stressful times a lot easier to swallow.

    If there is anything I can do, don't hesitate to call me. You are in my prayers and thoughts and those of so many who share in your sorrow.

Sincerely,

Jamie Herdon

Follow-Up Letter to an Interview:

Dear Mr. Smith:

It was a pleasure meeting you at the interview on Friday. Pepsico is a great company with great people. It's easy to see why your firm is growing in market share internationally.

Per your request, enclosed is the information regarding my experience at Jiffy Incorporated. As you will see, I gained practical experience and knowledge in the areas you're concerned with. I believe that I can help Pepsico achieve the growth it desires.

If there are any questions or comments do not hesitate to call me at (909) 884-2354.

Sincerely,

Amy Catch

Letter of Rejection:

Dear Mr. Smith:

Thank you for your application for the Sales Manager's position in our branch office. After careful review, I regret to inform you that you were not chosen for the position. However, should other opportunities become available we will keep your application on file and notify you should you be a candidate.

Again, thank you for your interest in Computer Specialists.

Sincerely,

Tracy McDonald, Director
Human Resources

FIGURE 1

Example of a Full-Block Formatted Letter

January 2, 2001

Mr. Barry Knight, Marketing Director
San Manuel Bingo and Casino
530 W. 57th Street
Little Bend, PA 10019

Dear Mr. Knight:

Recently, per your request, you should have received a copy of my proposal along with my press kit for consideration for conducting the seminar.

Enclosed are additional ideas for the seminar. One other idea centers around ethics. Focusing on several strategies that have the potential of significantly affecting the interview process, these strategies can be applied to sales situation. The topic not only focuses on such psychological influences as mirroring and neurolinguistic programming, but also color and dress.

I look forward to working with you and will call in the next ten days regarding possibilities for the seminar. If there are any questions or comments do not hesitate to call me at (909) 792-0002.

Sincerely,

Patricia Hampton, Ph.D.

Enclosure

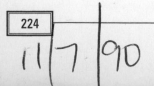

FIGURE 2

Example of a Modified-Block Formatted Letter

August 17, 2001

Mr. Frank Neighbors
A Different Kind of Touch Florists
110 N. Carpenter Street
Farmers Point, MA 02113

Dear Mr. Neighbors:

Thank you for your recent letter of inquiry. Enclosed are materials you requested regarding the flower arranging segment that was featured on *KNBC Morning Show* on January 25.

By using a mixture of dry and fresh flowers and plants you can further the life of a flower arrangement. Furthermore, you can adapt different flowers and plants for different holidays. This type of arrangement would be an excellent addition to your floral offerings.

Again, thank you for inquiry. If there are comments or questions do not hesitate to call me at (909) 793-0023.

Sincerely,

Marianne L. Snow
Flowers for a Difference

Enclosure

FIGURE 3

Example of a Semi-Block Formatted Letter

June 30, 2001

Mr. Brad Phillips
41040 Millcreek Crossing Street
Palm Springs, CA 92387

Dear Mr. Phillips:

Thank you for your interest in Donovan Pools and Sidings. Enclosed is the material you requested for review, as well as a video regarding the benefits of our products to enhancing the value of your home. Regarding our pools, experts can help you develop a pool area that will be the source of enjoyment with family and friends for years to come. In addition, we specialize in vinyl siding that is guaranteed for life. Just think, never having to paint your home again!

Donovan has been in the business of making houses—homes since 1956. We have been featured in *Home and Garden, Ladies Home Journal,* and *Architectual Digest,* as offering high quality products for the home. If you have additional questions or wish to make an appointment with one of our service specialists, call us at 1-888-989-POOL.

We look forward to serving you.

Respectfully yours,

Debra Mitchell
Regional Manager
Donovan Pools and Siding

DM/mc

EXERCISE

Using the tips given in this chapter, write a thank you note to someone that has done a favor for you in business. If you just met someone that would enhance your professional network, write a letter to let them know that it was a pleasure to meet them.

EXERCISE

TWENTY-SEVEN

International Savvy at Home and Abroad

The world has truly shrunk in size given electronic mail, fast air travel, and the influence of world economies on our homeland. Business is global these days, sourcing for parts and merchandise outside our own boundaries to make products and create services that are sold in America and around the world.

Americans traveling abroad have picked up a bad reputation as being ugly in their behavior and attitude—demanding McDonald's-style food and criticizing cultures that have been around far longer than our mere 200 plus years existence. Rather than appreciate the difference, demands are made to maintain the American status quo in foreign lands. One of the reasons why the Japanese were so successful in business in the seventies and eighties was due to how they handled the people they met in the global community.

Foreigners coming to America for business or pleasure often maintain much of their culture, while incorporating the things that make the United States one of the richest countries in the world. In the political arena, the U.S. President is responsible for entertaining foreign dignitaries with the hope of resolving issues between countries. How do they handle foreign guests in a manner that promotes positive rapport and fosters relationships? Yes, there are unique ways to handle foreign visitors, unlike our native guests, that will promote profitable business relationships. In this chapter we will discuss ways to entertain foreign guests and dignitaries as well as give tips for success in your business travels abroad.

The best tip to be successful entertaining foreign guests is to read about the country and get an understanding of the culture. This will enhance your sensitivity and appreciation for the differences between cultures and better prepare you for successful entertaining. Have an open mind about people from different cultures and avoid stereotyping them one way or another. For example, not all Latin Americans take a siesta in the afternoon. Further, all Asians are not the same: Thai people are very different from Vietnamese; and Chinese are very different from Japanese. Moreover, people from Britain, Ireland, and Scotland are not all English. They are British, Scottish, and Irish and are all very different. Finally, Britains and Australians speak English, but they are very different from Americans. By reading about people from different cultures, you can appreciate the differences.

Handling Foreign Guests

Whether your foreign guest is staying at your home or at a hotel, make an impression by having a basket of fruit or flowers placed in his/her room. When choosing flowers, avoid white or yellow if your guests are Chinese or Middle Eastern. Also, if dealing with Europeans, avoid chrysanthemums since they are linked with death. Moreover, consider helping them when they are making arrangements to visit by recommending or handling restaurants, hotels, airports, and transportation accommodations.

When someone visits you from a foreign country don't assume that they will want to eat their country's food during their stay. Rather, choose restaurants that have a continental menu that pleases most palates. Although we consider squid or sea urchin strange foods abroad, many foreigners consider corn on the cob, grits, and hot dogs strange. Other foods that are considered strange include sweet potatoes, pumpkin and pecan pies, and marshmallows.

If entertaining people who are Muslim or Jewish, depending on the extent that they follow the rules of their religion, operate from the standpoint that they are orthodox or conservative and follow their religious beliefs closely regarding food and other practices. For example, Muslims do not drink alcohol and they do not eat foods such as lobster, pigs, goats, and birds. Moreover, they don't eat foods prepared with oils or other parts of these animal. Jews cannot have milk and meat in the same container. Further, meat and fowl must be kosher, which is prepared under religious guidelines.

Also be aware that your foreign guests operate on a different meal plan compared to Americans. For most Americans the main meal is at night and is called dinner. For most countries abroad the main meal is at noon with a light meal late in the evening such as nine or ten o'clock. You may try to work within these confines while they are visiting or perhaps discuss with them how they want to schedule their meals.

If dealing with business people from Latin America, Asia, or the Middle East, include your family in selected activities outside business. Getting to know the family is part of building trust in the relationship and subsequently closing the deal. Compared to conducting business with other Americans, foreign business deals take more time to allow for the relationship to grow. You will find that people from such foreign countries as Brazil, Spain, and Saudi Arabia will stand close to you and perhaps hug you. Don't step back, they will just get close to you again. Also, be wary of the use of hand gestures such as "V" for victory or okay since these are interpreted as insults abroad. Further, avoid propping up your foot so that the sole of your shoe is showing. This is considered rude in most Asian and Middle Eastern countries. Try to limit your hand gestures when dealing with foreign guests to avoid mishaps. However, when dealing with guests from Scandinavian countries, Canada, Germany, or Switzerland, business is conducted in a similar fashion to Americans.

When greeting foreign guests be aware of the differences that exist in our culture and theirs. In America we extend our hand and shake the other person's while looking straight into their eyes. You may consider looking above their eyes since most foreigners, such as Asians, avoid direct eye contact. You may also want to incorporate a slight bow to the head to accompany your hand shake when dealing with Asian guests.

When entertaining foreign guests, avoid taking them to places of questionable taste such as a strip joint or a belly dancing Greek restaurant. Rather, choose entertainment that is conservative such as tickets to a sports event or a world renowned singer such as Julio Iglesias. If you live near a casino, gambling is not an option. It may offend someone's personal beliefs and religion. Moreover, don't invite them to church unless they invite themselves.

When it comes to giving gifts to your foreign visitors, consider items with a company logo. Avoid gifts that are expensive and imply sexual overtones since these will be considered bribery or in poor taste. Items that are suitable for placing a corporate logo include executive diaries, tie clips, lapel pins, key chains, scarves, pen and pencil sets, and credit or business card cases. Some other gifts that are suitable include champagne (if they drink alcohol), crystal paper weights, or silver letter openers.

Many times guests will bring a present and offer it to you as a way of saying thank you. Please accept it graciously. However, if dealing with someone from an Arab country they will expect a gift in return so be prepared. Make sure to give it to them in front of their associates so the gesture is not construed as a bribe.

Another issue is calling a foreign guest by his or her first name. Many Americans have gotten too relaxed with this and should wait until the other person gives permission to do so whether it is in America or anywhere else. Particularly with foreign guests it is considered an insult and damages the image that foreigners have of us in business.

If handling foreign guests who don't speak English at all or very well, hire a translator. Usually they will be listed in the *Yellow Pages* or you can contact the local embassy or consulate for guidance. If this is your first time hiring such an individual, you may want to talk to friends regarding a recommendation or check with the Better Business Bureau for those listed in the local directory.

Also if you conduct business with people of one specific foreign you may consider having your business cards made up with an English version on one side and the other language on the other. When I traveled to Thailand, the lawyer whom I dealt with had his business cards written in Thai on one side and English on the other.

Etiquette Abroad

Many of the issues discussed in handling foreign visitors apply to traveling abroad. First and foremost, read up on the country that you're visiting.

Understand the culture, get an idea of the language, history, and food. Appreciate and look forward to the differences as a way to expand your knowledge of the world.

If going to a country where English is not spoken, don't assume that you will have a translator or that someone in the company will speak English. Most times this will be handled but still understand how to say some of the key words such as "please," "thank you," "good morning," and "restroom." You might want to carry a dictionary that will help you translate and/or have arrangements made prior to your stay and have a translator available. English may be the language of the world, yet it may not be the language spoken among the people with whom you're conducting business.

As with handling foreign guests in the states, conducting business abroad is different. For example, often conducting the business at hand will not be done immediately but perhaps in a couple of days. The people whom you're visiting will have to get to know you and build their trust with you prior to conducting business. Don't get frustrated—this is just how it is. You may be introduced to the person's family and associates before the subject of business is ever brought up.

Further, you will find that promptness is not the rule in many countries. When conducting business in such parts of the world as Asia, Latin America, and the Middle East, expect to be kept waiting when you show up on time to the meeting. However, it is considered rude to be doing something else while you're waiting because it is interpreted as more important than the business at hand. However, in Germany, Switzerland, and the Scandinavian countries, punctuality is sincerely appreciated. In Spain and Portugal, the workday does not start until ten o'clock and lunch is served around two o'clock.

Gift giving is common practice when visiting a foreign country. Understand what types of gifts are appropriate in that country before running out and buying something that will be an embarrassment to you and the receiver. Be sure that the gift is not overly expensive or it will be interpreted as a bribe or something that is questionable in taste. Some gift ideas include T-shirts with a famous sports team name on it, framed museum and concert posters, or items from famous stores such as Bloomingdales and Saks Fifth Avenue. As well, consider gifts with your company's logo and name imprinted on them such as paper weights, pen and pencil sets, and desksets. Avoid giving clocks to the Chinese, knives to Latins, or handkerchiefs or statues of dogs or pets to Middle Easterners. These have negative connotations and should be avoided. You might also consider flowers but realize that different flowers and their colors have different meanings in different countries

If staying at a business associate's home abroad, bring gifts for the children if they are present, as well as the spouse. Some ideas for such gifts include toys, books, and games.

When presenting the gift, give it after business has been conducted in China. In Russia, gifts are exchanged during toasts made at dinner. If in an Arab nation or Japan, wait till your host gives you a gift before presenting yours. Be sure that the gift is presented in front of others so as to not be interpreted as a bribe. Often the Japanese will not open the gift in front of you—this is out of respect. Further, avoid using brightly colored wrapping paper to cover the gift, go with a conservative muted pattern.

For a woman traveling abroad to conduct business, gift giving is a touchy situation. Go for more impersonal gifts such as an executive diary, pen set, or paper weight. Otherwise, particularly in countries where women are rarely seen in the workplace, personal gifts may be interpreted as more than friendship.

Further, if you are a women traveling to Arab countries, be aware of your dress and modify accordingly. In Saudi Arabia women are covered from head to toe. This is not the place to be wearing short skirts, short sleeved or sleeveless tops, deep necklines, and such. You may be expected to cover up as a matter of respect but don't wear pants. In Thailand and other Asian countries where Hindu or Buddhism is practiced do not wear pants to the temples. Most often they will not let you in. In Egypt, men and women wear both western and their national dress—the caftan. Women will often cover their head, in addition to their body, in black as a matter of respect. For women, as for men, dress conservatively and more formally than you might at home when conducting business abroad.

For men, wear dark suits with white shirts and modest ties to create the necessary rapport. Although, white shirts are common for men, women should avoid white or winter white dresses, suits, and shoes since white is the color of mourning in some countries.

As in entertaining foreign visitors in the States, when traveling abroad be sensitive to your body language; particularly hand gestures and eye contact, which vary from country to country. For example, the okay sign in the U.S. is an insult in many foreign countries as well as the "V" for victory sign. Direct eye contact is not made in Asian countries so don't try to look at the person all the time or try getting them to look at you—it's out of respect that they don't give you direct eye contact.

Speaking about gestures, usually Americans will automatically extend their hand no matter where they are when it comes to business. However, in Japan, although they are accustomed to American ways, wait till they extend their hand and slightly bow your head during the greeting.

In countries abroad you will be exposed to a variety of new foods and drinks. Some of these you won't care to ever order but as the guest, allow your host to recommend the dishes. Most times they will take into account the differences that exist between your country and theirs. However, if you get something that you don't like, don't make an issue of it. Rather, cut the food into tiny pieces and move it about your plate to give the impression that you've eaten it.

As mentioned earlier, in many countries the main meal is at noon followed by a light late dinner. In countries such as Brazil, Argentina, and Spain the evening meal starts at around nine or ten o'clock. You may consider having a snack to be able to hold out for such a late meal. The British have tea about four in the afternoon. This is not "high tea." This is a time to relax, conduct business, and to snack a bit so as to be able to hold out for dinner at a later time. During tea time, pound cake, scones, and small tea sandwiches are served.

In China, Thailand, and Japan, you will be served lots of food buffet style but try each different dish without gorging on your favorite. There will be plenty more to come. Do not eat or drink until your host does and don't leave the table to conclude the meal before them.

In France, although you may be an expert at picking wines, allow them to do so. They believe they are the experts. Most business is conducted in France over lunch or dinner and breakfast meetings are nonexistent. In Italy, the meal is served differently with the pasta or antipasto served first, followed by the main course, and then salad. In India, it is customary to wash your hands and mouth before eating.

Although Greeks love doing business over coffee and ouzo (a liqueur), and the Chinese make lots of toasts, watch the alcohol. The beer is stronger in Germany as well as the sake in Japan and the ouzo in Greece. As in conducting business in America, getting drunk abroad will not make a deal but more than likely kill it. In France, wine is part of every meal; however, if you have a low tolerance for alcohol, drink bottled water. It is not necessary to accept nor drink alcoholic beverages that are offered to you while abroad. If at a dinner party and wine is served don't drink it. If champagne is served and a toast is made to seal a deal, just raise your glass but don't partake.

When traveling abroad, view the cultural differences with an open mind and appreciate the change of pace. Remember that trying to fit someone into a stereotype is like a foreigner saying that all Americans ride horses and wear cowboy hats. Also, because you are making the effort to try to understand a culture, your efforts will be appreciated even if you make a lot of mistakes or confess your ignorance.

If you have not traveled to a foreign country, plan to do so. Not only will you get an appreciation of a different way of life, you will further appreciate all the great things that America has to offer.

EXERCISE

EXERCISE

If you are planning to make a trip to a foreign country or will be hosting foreign visitors, read up on that country's history, customs, and language. Understand and appreciate the differences and try to incorporate some of the above mentioned practices in your business transactions.

TWENTY-EIGHT

Hi-Tech Etiquette

We live in a world of instant communication and information over-load. Through the Internet, information is at our fingertips. Through pagers, cell phones, electronic mail (e-mail), and faxes, communication is instantaneous. "I'll e-mail you," is commonly heard at the tale end of many phone conversations. In fact e-mail is overtaking the phone call as a means of communication. Why? Especially for long distance corre-spondence, e-mail is less expensive and sometimes quicker, with messages traveling 3,000 miles a minute. But is it the right way to communicate with prospective and current clients, prospective employees and officials? What is the best way to communicate in this era of instant communication and tech-nology overload?

There are several issues that need to be discussed before getting specific. First of all, is the issue of privacy in communication. If communicating con-fidential or sensitive information be aware that e-mail, faxes, and telephone lines are not secure. We've all heard the stories or watched the movies of computer hackers breaking into government or company computer systems and being able to retrieve sensitive information. That is a possibility; how-ever, companies don't need to hire hackers to monitor employee electronic correspondence—it's already built into the system.

Many companies monitor conversations as a matter of evaluating cus-tomer service, routinely tap into employees e-mail, and who knows who sees the messages faxed at the machine down the hall. You say that's illegal. The bottom line to many companies today is that you're on their time—so they can do whatever they want. Many times when calling my insurance company a recording comes on that points out that the call may be monitored. Whether the recording is there or not, evaluate the need for privacy when determining appropriate vehicles to deliver the message. Even with cell phones, the technology is available to monitor and to tap into numbers called. So if you're job hunting and need to send your resume, think twice about sending it through the company Internet system or fax. If it gets into the wrong hands it may spell big trouble for you.

Another issue that needs attention is the level of computer or technological sophistication that you possess and that of the individual that you're trying to reach. If you're with a software company, it is expected that you would use hi-tech means of communication. However, if you're the computer guru and the individual you are trying to talk with is not, try more traditional forms of communication like a phone call. Evaluate the means most employed by the other person and use that means as a way to communicate. Ask that person which way is best to reach them.

In business, meetings are part of the job description; and client meetings are the key to sales success. What is the best way to contact a client or prospective client to set up the meeting? If having lunch with a friend or a prospective employee, what is the best way to set the date and confirm it? The best way is by phone or in person. Voice contact is essential when setting up important meetings with individuals outside the company. Why? Suppose you do call and leave a voice message, e-mail, or fax them, they can claim they never got it. Moreover, unless the person is constantly on a computer or attached to a fax machine, they may never get the message or get it too late. Furthermore, when confirming a meeting time, always do it by phone and either talk to that individual or to their assistant. Do not leave a voice message, e-mail, or fax confirmation. More than likely the person will not get it in time or at all. If you cannot make a meeting do not e-mail, leave a voice message, or fax this information. What it communicates is that you don't keep commitments and you're too afraid to face the music when bowing out. Moreover, these ways do not always provide the opportunity to set up another time to meet—which may be what you're trying to avoid.

Moreover, don't try to conduct new business with clients over voice mail, fax, or e-mail. Face-to-face contact is essential in communicating your expertise and the quality of your company. Sometimes when telemarketing for leads, in the initial conversation information is exchanged and/or sent, faxed, or e-mailed. However, in this situation the prospective client is expecting the information and knows how it will be delivered. But in closing the deal, face-to-face contact is essential. In dealing with current clients, such as reorders of products or services, this can be communicated through mail, e-mail, fax, or voice mail.

When dealing with friends outside of the business arena, using voice messages, e-mail, or fax is fine. However, it is suggested that you contact them on their home computer, fax, or home phone. Even if having lunch with a friend during the work week, contact them on their home communication devices. This may avoid any embarrassment or reprimand at work.

Now, what if you've been invited to the company party or get together with clients at a colleagues home. First and foremost it is imperative that you R.S.V.P. whether or not you're coming and if you are bringing a guest. However, how you communicate this information can be through e-mail, a voice message, or by fax. It gives a more personal touch when you call and talk to the host yourself rather than the other means. Many times company parties are advertised through e-mail or flyers, so it's fine to deliver your R.S.V.P. through impersonal means as well.

However, if you're having a party for a client at your home or restaurant, do you send invitations by e-mail, fax, or voice message? None of the above. Either call the client and those you wish to invite and invite them personally or send invitations. The other means, although easier and quicker, are too impersonal. If you're having a party with your friends, how you inform them is up to you. If you've been invited by friends to join them, do let them know whether you're planning to attend through any means you can before the date.

Now let's go to the next level. How do you handle your communication devices when in a meeting or riding with a client in the car? May I suggest that whether you're meeting with a current client, prospective client, a recruit in a job interview, or meeting a friend, don't bring your cell phone. And turn off your pager. If you're expecting an important message and you're wearing your pager—put it on vibrator mode. When conducting a seminar it is distracting when pagers go off as well as cell phones. It's not cool and really doesn't say anything good about you if you're constantly being beeped or called while in a meeting. In fact, most business people or company recruiters consider it rude, a distraction, and will probably not want anything to do with you. So don't bring your cell phone to a meeting or interview and put your pager on vibrator mode if you're expecting an important call. Moreover, if you're in the meeting and get paged, do not make a production of reading the number. Excuse yourself and glance at it. But remember the person that you are with is the most important person right now so don't get distracted with communicating to others.

If the call is important, then ask the person that you are with if you may take a moment to return the call and make the call in the restroom or out-side the meeting room. But please don't do this throughout your meeting. Furthermore, if you happen to carry your cell phone with you to the meeting (and I hope it doesn't ring) do not make calls on it unless they deal directly with the business at hand. For example, if you need to check product prices or media availability then it is appropriate to use the phone. If you happen to get a call, let the person on the phone know that you are in a meeting and that you will call them back. Bottom line, don't take your cell phone or pager with you to meetings or job interviews. You may be ruining any chance of getting the business or job.

Many times I've been with people or have seen people that are constantly on their cell phones during lunch or meetings, and it sends the message that you're avoiding them or want to be perceived as important. Bottom line, you are being inconsiderate to the person you are with. Furthermore, if you think this action is saying that you're important, think again. What it's really saying is that you lack self-confidence.

When riding in a car (whether driving or as a passenger) or traveling on business, what is the appropriate use of cell phones, lap tops, and other high-tech communication vehicles? Regarding driving and using the cell phone, many phone companies are now saying to use the device with cau-tion when driving. Please do, particularly if you are carrying passengers, and limit your calls when you're driving alone.

Avoid taking personal or business calls when riding with a business col-league in the car. If someone is returning a call that pertains to the business at hand then make it brief. The cell phone should be used for communi-cating important information such as family emergencies and/or business decisions, not talking with friends.

Answering machines may be considered antique, but the recording tells a lot about your image. Although they truly make life easier, whether at home or at the office be sensitive to the recording that tells callers to leave a message. Forget the jungle music unless you're the San Diego Zoo and avoid the chatter particularly if it's a business line or if you receive business calls at home. Indicate in your recording either the number, household, or business reached and tell the caller to leave a number, business and name, and the best time to be reached. Since many people work out of their home, it is important to either have a separate phone line for business or, if not possible, be sure that the recording is simple and to the point. Avoid having your five year old make the recording.

How about lap top computers during a business meeting? Unless it is part of the presentation, it's not necessary. Often salespersons will conduct a presentation with a prospective client, providing the information visually through the computer demonstration. The computer should be used as a visual aid, much like an overhead or slide projector but not the presentation itself. In addition to laptop computers are the hand-held executive diaries/pagers/computers. Again, don't be consumed with it during a meeting checking messages, dates, or sending messages. Wait until the meeting is over to input the information. Computers are part of our lives but they don't have to be our lives—personal contact is still the best way to conduct business.

If traveling by air, using your laptop while flying uses your time effectively; however if traveling with your boss, talk to him or her unless he or she is working on a computer. Further, avoid making calls on your cell phone or the airlines cell phone unless it is business that has to be decided on now or you need to contact family regarding a change in your arrival time. Don't use the phone to talk to friends all the time you're in the air. Besides being sorry when the bill arrives, it's annoying to the other passengers.

If you have felt uncomfortable when others have "played" with their high-tech toys in the name of business, then you know how they might feel if you do the same. The person that you are with, whether it is for business or pleasure, is the most important person at the time. Let them know that you are there for them and want their business by minimizing the use of cell phones, pagers, and laptops.

I personally don't have a cell phone, pager, laptop, or computer diary, and I survive very well. Unless it's a do or die situation, a phone call can always wait, and, the last time I checked, most situations, whether business or pleasure, were not to die for. A headhunter friend of mine does not have those devices either and is extremely successful. When he contacts his clients it is at his office and on the phone. When interviewing prospective recruits, the focus is on them, free of interruptions from calls, e-mails, or faxes.

In this high-tech world, face-to-face personal contact is still the best. In this world of information overload and instant communication, the speed of business may be faster but high touch interaction with others will seal the deal and enhance future business opportunities. Particularly when conducting business abroad, the format in which it is handled is very different than in America. In most cultures outside the U.S., business is conducted after everyone has gotten to know one another and their families face-to-face. Be sensitive to this and brush up on your personal communication skills when working on a global basis.

Moreover, the level of technology may not be as high as your company's and hence, more traditional forms of communication may be more appropriate. For example, whereas Americans are used to WebTV and 300 plus cable stations, there are less than twenty stations in Europe at this point and no WebTV. The Internet, although it is a world wide phenomena, is predominately an American enterprise. For example, it is predicted that shopping on the Internet will be about twenty-five percent of retail sales in the near future; however, this is in America. Only a small percentage of individuals in other countries are on-line. Hence, the foreign company that you're trying to contact may not be on-line or have a fax. So instead of getting absorbed by all of America's technological capabilities, read up on the country that you are dealing with and their technological know how before contacting them by e-mail.

Conducting business by fax, e-mail, and other high-tech ways are okay, just evaluate whether it is the best way to get something done. If you're talking to someone by phone you can alert them to a forthcoming fax or e-mail so there is better chance that they will get it. If you're concerned about privacy you may inquire if the fax is private.

Still, in developing long lasting business relationships, consider setting up a face-to-face meeting first. Once you've gotten to know one another then consider future correspondence by e-mail or other high-tech ways. Moreover, you might want to ask the person what is the best way to reach them. That will give you the information you need to communicate most effectively with them. If they say "e-mail me," you might want to call them first and let them know that you're sending a message by e-mail so they can look for it. If they don't get it, then it might indicate something wrong with their Internet server or the address given. If they are comfortable receiving faxes make sure to direct the fax to their attention with a cover letter. Again, because technology is not always working, call first so they know to expect it. Finally, to be on the safe side follow up with a hard copy sent through the mail if it's an important document.

Communication in this high-tech world is as easy as ever. Use today's technological advances as a means to better communicate to customers and prospective clients. To summarize here are tips to high-tech etiquette:

- Avoid bringing cell phones and pagers to meetings.
- If wearing a pager, put it on vibrator mode.
- Evaluate the level of privacy needed in determining modes for communication.
- Ask clients the best method for reaching them.
- Confirm meetings by personal contact or leave a message with the assistant.
- Invite clients to meetings or get togethers by personal contact or written invitation.
- Limit cell phone use while in the car or in the air.
- Use laptop computers only as visual components of a presentation.
- Avoid making or taking calls during meetings unless it deals with the business at hand.
- Do not bring a pager or cell phone to an interview.
- Inform customers of forthcoming faxes or e-mail messages and follow up with a hard copy in the mail.
- Do not initiate new business contacts through e-mail or fax.

- When developing communication with foreign companies, evaluate their level of technological sophistication prior to sending messages via high-tech vehicles.
- Minimize the use of hand-held executive diaries/pagers/computers until after a client meeting.
- Face-to-face meetings are the best way to close a deal.

EXERCISE

For one week, try to incorporate the tips in communicating with clients and associates. Limit use of your cell phone and pager and contact clients personally by phone.

Maintaining Your Investment

If putting together a wardrobe is essential to creating the executive image that's right for you, maintaining your investment is just as essential, if not more so. Why? Because the cost of apparel continues to increase as its durability continues to decrease. Shirt buttons fall off shortly after purchase. Hems fall out of skirts, jacket linings tear, items fade; the list goes on and on.

Maintaining your wardrobe is crucial to making your investment count. Let's say a button falls off the jacket of your favorite suit. You put it back in your closet without fixing it. An important meeting comes up and you want to wear the suit, but it needs mending. Don't let this happen to you! Maintain your wardrobe and you'll always be ready to go.

When caring for your wardrobe, be thorough. Start with hangers. They should be made of plastic, wood, or padded fabric. Avoid wire hangers and hangers that are too short; these do not maintain garment shape. Above all, avoid hanging knit garments. They should be stored on a shelf or in a drawer. However, if you must hang a knit garment, fold it and place it over two padded rods or hangers to minimize the amount of sag and to save the knit from stretching out of shape.

When storing clothing, avoid plastic bags. Instead, try to purchase garment bags in fabrics like cotton that allow the clothing to breathe during storage. Clean items before storing. Fruit juice stains fade garments over time, and food stains attract moths. As an alternative to mothballs, purchase paradichlorobenzene in prewrapped packages. When storing wool garments during the summer seasons, choose cool areas or send them to the local dry cleaner or retailer for cold storage.

Choosing and Caring for Fibers

Here's a look at some basic care considerations for the main types of fibers available in today's marketplace.

Wool

Whether it's winter, spring, summer, or fall, wool is the fiber for all seasons. Hard to imagine? With today's technology in yarns and weaves, wool can be worn year-round. Being a smart shopper of wool and considerate of the care of your garments will make you a well dressed executive.

Begin by remembering what purpose the fiber is designed for. Consider what you expect in performance from the money, time, and effort invested in your purchase. With the endless array of textures, designs, and fabrics available, it's difficult to judge the quality of wool by hand; however, the Wool Products Labeling Act helps us to categorize these products easily.

Virgin wool is new wool that has never been used previously.

Pure wool or *100% wool* is a product using fabric composed completely of wool and is also new. However, the product as a whole may also be composed of 5% other fibers (typically in the lining).

Wool product means any product that contains virgin, reprocessed, or reused wool in some portion.

Reprocessed wool is wool that has been manufactured before but then reduced to fibers for reuse. The wool, however, has not been worn or used before.

Reused wool is reclaimed wool that has been manufactured and used by the consumer, then returned to a fibrous state and blended with stronger wools. Reused wool is often blended with other fabrics for the qualities known only to wool.

The *Woolmark* symbol represents a quality-tested product manufactured from pure wool. It identifies wool that has met standards by the manufacturer and assures you that the wool product you are buying is of the highest quality. Additional information is not necessary when this symbol is present. The next time you're shopping, ask the salesperson to point out the *Wool-mark* symbol.

Be aware to check these aspects of the product before buying:

- The drape and hang. Wool fabrics should feel springy and elastic, yet soft; they should also feel fuzzy, except for worsted wools which are smooth. When choosing wool, drape the fabric in bias folds, then in straight folds, to find out how the garment will hang.
- Does the wool fabric hold pleats and creases?
- Resiliency or wrinkle resistance. Crush a small part of the fabric in your hand, then release. Good wool springs back into shape almost immediately with no wrinkling. (That's why wool garments are great for travel.)
- Surface quality. Woolen fabrics have a soft, uneven surface, with little sheen, except for worsted wools, which have a clean, even smooth, lustrous surface. Wool gabardine is a worsted wool.
- The weave, or pick. A good-quality worsted wool has a clear outline of the weave and is uniform and compact.

Why buy wool? Wool has a variety of characteristics that synthetics have yet to achieve. Here are some of the qualities that make wool ideal for suits, jackets, skirts, and pants.

- It is flexible and elastic.
- It repels moisture making it resistant to accidental spills, yet absorbs perspiration.
- It is resilient, making it ideal for travel.
- It keeps its shape and good looks for a longer period of time than a 100% synthetic product.
- It can bounce back to its original shape after being pulled or stretched.
- It is naturally flame-retardant.
- It is versatile. No other fiber can be spun or woven in such varieties of weight and texture.
- It absorbs dyes easily and beautifully.

- It has an excellent ability to insulate, keeping you warm in the winter.
- It breathes, allowing the body's moisture to pass through so you can stay cool in the summer.

Wool takes a minimal amount of care. Follow these simple guidelines and your wool garments will last for years.

- Give clothes a twenty-four-hour rest between wearings.
- Empty pockets and remove belts before hanging them to rest.
- Fold wool knitwear and store in drawers or shelves.
- Brush wool pieces lengthwise with a still brush. Use a damp sponge for your knits or finer wools.
- To refresh wools, simply hang them in a steamy bathroom. Any wrinkle will fall out with steam.
- Store winter wools carefully during the summer. Include mothballs or cedar chips to keep your woolens free from moths, silverfish, and other insects.
- Follow care instructions carefully. Most wool garments should be dry-cleaned, but only once or twice a year. Over-dry-cleaning will dry out the fibers and fade color as well.
- If you choose to hand-wash your wool sweaters, use Woolite or a mild liquid soap. When using Woolite, follow the directions for soaking time explicitly.
- Wool, cashmere, or lambswool sweaters can be hand-washed or dry-cleaned. Angora, however, is extremely fragile and must be professionally dry-cleaned.

Silk

Silk, like wool, is a highly popular fabric. One of the most luxurious natural fibers available, it has long been prized for its strength, beauty, and versatility.

Silk is produced from the larvae of moths. The larva, or silkworm, prepares its cocoon by extruding a liquid that solidifies in the air into silk filaments. These filaments are unwound from the cocoon and processed into silk yarns.

Silk is a natural-protein fiber. Filaments are fine and long and can measure from 1,000 to as long as 3,000 yards. Silk is smooth, with a high luster and sheen, but is most noted for its strength.

Silk has good elastic recovery, allowing it to preserve its shape over time. Its wrinkle recovery is good, although not as good as wool's; creases will hang out partially but not completely.

Silk is highly absorbent and can be brilliantly dyed. This property also makes it cool for summer wear; however, perspiration will weaken and damage the fibers. Since silk is a protein fiber it has some of the same characteristics as wool. Although it burns when placed in a flame, it will not continue to burn if the flame is removed.

When it comes to buying silk, there are different grades or qualities available. Test a garment before buying by squeezing it in your hand. A good-quality silk bounces back instantly.

Caring for silk requires caution in the kinds of laundry products used. Silk is damaged by strong alkalis and dissolves in caustic soda, but soap, borax, and ammonia cause little damage. Cleaning solvents and spot removers are also safe.

Avoid chlorine bleaches; however, hydrogen peroxide and perborate (all-fabric) bleaches can be used without damage to the fiber. Dry-cleaning is recommended for most silks, but some are washable. Use a mild soap or synthetic detergent, warm water, and minimum handling. Protein shampoos are also recommended, since silk is a protein fabric. Swish the garment in soapy water for about three minutes. For soiled areas, apply extra detergent with the palm of the hand, rubbing in a circular fashion. Rinse garments in cold water. You may wish to put a capful of vinegar in the rinse water to extract any alkali residue left by the soap. Do not wring out excess water. Roll the garment in a towel, then hang it up to dry away from the sunlight. You may also lay it on a towel, smoothing it to prevent wrinkles, then hang it on a plastic hanger to air dry away from sunlight. Sunlight damages silk.

Most problems with silk have to do with color. Should you choose a dramatically colored silk garment, test it to make sure it doesn't run. The more intense the color, the less stable the dye—and the more likely it is to fade with perspiration or sunlight and to run when cleaned.

When pressing silk, use a medium-to-low ironing temperature. You could also turn it face down while the fabric is still damp and press it with a steam iron. A steamer is also acceptable for removing wrinkles. Silk scorches or yellows at temperatures of 300°F or higher.

When wearing silk blouses or shirts, avoid deodorants and antiperspirants that contain aluminum chloride. If perspiration is a problem, wear protective dress shields.

Ramie

Perhaps you've purchased something blended with ramie and wondered what kind of fiber it was. With the new-found popularity of this fiber, some explanations are in order.

Ramie is a bast fiber akin to linen, cotton, and jute. Often referred to as China Grass, ramie has been cultivated in the Orient for hundreds of years. Nowadays, it is commercially grown in China, Japan, Egypt, France, Italy, Indonesia, and Russia.

Ramie, like cotton and linen, is a natural cellulosic fiber. The fibers are long, sometimes more than eighteen inches in length, and, though fine, are extremely strong, especially when pulled. Fibers are white, lustrous, and silk-like in appearance. Unfortunately, they rate poorly in elongation and elastic properties.

Ramie can resemble fine linen or can be heavy and coarse, like canvas. It is often used in shirts, table coverings, and napkins but is increasingly found in all kinds of clothing.

The care of ramie should closely match the care of linen. Dry-cleaning suits it best. Although ramie can be machine-washed if blended with synthetics such as polyester, be sure to follow the care instructions closely.

Like linen (but unlike synthetics), ramie won't melt or burn under high ironing temperatures. Use the linen or cotton temperature settings when ironing.

Ramie reacts to chemicals in a similar way to linen or cotton. It is not easily damaged by cold-concentrate mineral acids. It is also resistant to microorganisms, insects, and rotting. Gradual loss of strength does occur when the fiber is exposed to sunlight, but the damage is minimal, particularly when sunlight is filtered through window glass.

Ramie is highly absorbent, making it a good choice for summer apparel.

Acrylic

Dupont developed acrylic fiber during the late forties. It has been advertised as a fiber with the warmth of wool—without the itch. Used extensively in all kinds of clothing, it is particularly effective for sweaters and other winter clothing—especially if you happen to be allergic to wool.

What makes acrylic so special? In the first place, it is resilient. Bulky fabrics made of acrylic retain their shape. The moisture regain of acrylic is relatively low, resulting in speedy drying; hence, this fiber is ideal for skiwear.

Acrylic fibers also have good elastic recovery, so garments maintain their shape after laundering. With proper care this fiber shows little dimensional change (such as shrinkage); however, excess heat and steam will cause the fabric to shrink and to lose bulk.

Acrylic is resistant to weak alkalies, but strong ones degrade it, as do concentrated acids. Bleaches, detergents, and cleaning solvents are all safe.

Acrylics are resistant to sunlight, meaning that clothing can be dried outside. Unlike wool, they will not be harmed by mildew and common household pests.

This fiber can be made into warm, bulky apparel without the weight, the itch, and the laundering hassles that accompany wool and other natural fibers. Look for domestic tradenames like Acrilan, Bi-Loft, Creslan, Orlon, Zefran, and Fina, or foreign-made Acribel, Townflower, Courtelle, Crylor, Dralon, Dolan, Leacril, Cashmilon, and Toraylon. When in doubt, look for the generic name "acrylic."

Acrylics are excellent for skiwear, children's snowsuits, and sport shirts. Deep-pile fabrics maintain their resiliency when blended with acrylic. For home sewers, acrylics have good wash-and-wear properties and will take permanent pleats and creases if heat-set properly.

Modacrylics

Fake furs are today's fashion focus for many designers. They look as real as the animal coats they imitate. But what are they made of? Surprisingly, a synthetic—modacrylic.

Modacrylic was first introduced in 1950 by the Union Carbide Corporation. The fiber was originally developed to withstand higher temperatures than other fibers. You might be more familiar with the use of modacrylics in children's wear: modacrylics are flame-resistant.

Modacrylics' other properties include strength and resilience. It has good elastic recover, but does not absorb moisture well, so it is not recommended for summer apparel. This fiber is also resistant to most alkalis and acids. Cleaning solvents do not damage it, but acetone, found in nail polish remover and other paint solvents, does.

Some common uses for modacrylic fibers, in addition to those already mentioned, include blankets, knitted goods, wigs and hairpieces, draperies, carpets, and industrial fabrics. These fibers can also be made into soft, resilient fabrics for clothes that retain their shape after washing. Modacrylic fibers and blends can be machine-washed and dried at home. (Set the dryer temperature on low to prevent shrinkage.) Modacrylics can also be dry-cleaned safely.

Look for these domestic tradenames: Verel, SEF, and Acrilan modacrylic. Kanekalon, from Japan, is often used to manufacture wigs.

Rayon

Rayon is another popular fabric in America's fashion houses. Blended with other fabrics, such as wool, silk, and linen, it provides an all-season choice for consumers. Rayon gabardines are particularly good for summer-weight suits and jackets. Rayon breathes, meaning it keeps you cool in hot weather.

Rayon absorbs dyes well and is quite economical. Part natural and part synthetic, it is made by chemically treating cellulosic fibers. Washable rayons are stronger and more shrink-resistant than regular rayons. Tradenames for rayon include Avril, Coloray, and Durvil.

Unfortunately, rayon has many weaknesses. Dry-clean only garments will shrink tremendously and lose shape if washed. Although rayon drapes well, it wrinkles at a moment's notice. Mildew damages it, so be sure to keep it in a cool, dry closet.

Follow the care instructions attached to your garment. If it says dry-clean only, then dry clean it only. Hand or machine washing will only ruin the garment. When ironing, use the perma press setting.

Cotton

Cotton is a natural cellulosic fiber. It is comfortable, soft, sturdy, and relatively inexpensive. One of the most important qualities of this fiber is that it breathes, which means that it absorbs moisture and perspiration, keeping you cool in warm weather. It also absorbs dyes well.

One problem with cotton is that it wrinkles easily. It can mildew if it is not kept in a dry area, and it is extremely flammable unless treated.

Fabric companies have developed techniques to enhance the good qualities of cotton and minimize its liabilities. Sanforized cotton is cotton that has been pre-shrunk. Sanfor-Set cotton is wrinkle resistant. Mercerized cotton has been strengthened and lusterized.

Most cottons are machine or hand-washable in cold, hot, or warm water. If garments are colored, wash them in cold water to retain the color. Most items can be machine-dried on the regular cycle with a warm setting. When ironing, use the steam setting. If you wish to use starch, feel free.

Linen

Linen is a natural fiber made from the flax plant. It is comfortable and breathable, making it a good choice for summer. It does not give off lint, is extremely durable, and resists heat, moths, and perspiration damage.

Wonderful as linen is, however, it does have several weaknesses. It wrinkles easily and holds creases poorly. It is also very expensive, although manufacturers have brought down the price and minimized wrinkling by blending it with polyester. Linen, like cotton, is extremely flammable.

Read care instructions diligently. Most linen items must be dry-cleaned professionally. When ironing, use the highest setting with steam.

Polyester

Polyester is one of today's wonder fibers. Busy lifestyles demand ease of care, and polyester, often blended with cotton or other natural fibers, offers freedom from shrinkage and ironing problems. It is machine washable and can be dried in an automatic drier on a regular setting. Like most synthetics, polyester will melt at high temperatures, so caution should be taken with ironing and washing temperature settings.

Polyester resists wrinkling, so it's great blended with cotton for shirts. A men's dress shirt in 65 to 70 percent cotton and 30 to 35 percent polyester gives the comfort of cotton with the ease of care and great looks of polyester.

Polyester is strong and resists mildew and moths. However, it does have its drawbacks. It is oliophilic, meaning it absorbs oil, and oil-based stains are difficult to remove through conventional washing methods. If you get an oil-based stain like salad dressing or grease, take the garment to the dry-cleaners immediately. They should be able to lift the stain. Another problem with polyester is that, like most synthetics, it does not breathe, causing clothing of 100 percent polyester to feel sticky and uncomfortable in warm climates. Furthermore, if the regular setting of your dryer is an extremely high temperature, it will soften the fabric and introduce permanent wrinkles. Remove polyester garments from the dryer when they are still damp and press them at once. This will help you to avoid over drying, which ages polyester and wards off the gradual shrinkage that occurs from over drying.

Some people are dead-set against polyester, which they associate with double-knit leisure suits. Through technology, however, we now have polyester that looks and feels like silk—with prices that approach it! Brands include Dacron, Fortel, and Kodel.

Nylon

Nylon is noted for strength without weight. It is highly resistant to abrasion, but this does not mean that clothing made of this fiber will never wear out. The garment's durability depends on the lifestyle of the wearer. Nylon fabric is silky and stretchable, yet rugged, making it ideal for bathing suits, windbreakers, and running apparel. As added benefits, it resists shrinkage, mildew, moths, and perspiration.

One drawback of nylon is the lack of moisture absorption, which can lead to a sticky feeling on the skin. For strength with the properties of natural fibers, try fabrics blended with nylon. Another drawback is nylon's tendency to pill. Pilling is the formation of tiny fuzz balls on the fabric surface. With synthetics these pills never fall off and must be clipped or sheared off.

Nylon also wrinkles, and when exposed to sunlight will become weak and damaged. It also burns and melts at high temperatures.

Look for tradenames like Anso, Antron, Celanese, and Quiana. Garments can be machine washed and dried, provided that the temperature setting on the dryer is not so high as to melt the fabric. Commercial dryers in particular, which often have extremely high temperature settings, have been known to melt nylon garments. When ironing, use a relatively low temperature setting. High temperatures will melt the fabric onto your iron and destroy it. Do not hang nylon items out in the sun to dry; such exposure will weaken the fiber.

Acetate

With its silk-like appearance, acetate is gorgeous in formal gowns. It is, however, a very delicate fiber. When exposed to sunlight over a period of time, acetate will fade. Use caution doing your nails while you are wearing acetate: this fiber disintegrates when fingernail polish remover is spilled on it. Acetate, a synthetic, does not breathe. It wrinkles and tears easily. It does not wash well, and, when exposed to a flame, burns easily and quickly.

However, acetate has many fine properties, including resistance to mildew, moths, and shrinkage. Because an acetate garment does not carry the price tag of a silk one, it is also economical.

Tradenames for acetate include Celanese, Ariloft, Avron, and Chromspun. Like rayon, acetate is part natural and part man made, produced by treating cellulosic fibers from soft wood trees with chemicals.

Follow the care label directions attached to your garment. Most acetate items must be professionally dry-cleaned. Set your iron on the lowest temperature setting to avoid burning or discoloring the garment. Triacetate, a close relation, possesses many of the same properties as acetate but is more heat resistant.

Fabric Know-How

In the preceding section we looked at the many different fibers available to home sewers and clothing consumers, exploring the assets and liabilities of each type. The next section will focus on fabric. What is a twill? What is a knit? And what is the best way to take care of them? Being an educated consumer will save you money and put you ahead in the wardrobe game—so read on for the inside scoop.

One of the basic elements of any fabric is weave. Most fabrics are created from one of three weaves, which vary in strength, durability, and appearance.

First is the plain weave, the most common method used in weaving fabrics. Plain weave fabrics include muslin, percale, print cloth, cheesecloth, chambray, gingham, batiste, organdy, linen, toweling, handkerchief linen, seersucker, challis, china silk, and some wool tweeds. Plain-woven fabrics are relatively inexpensive and durable.

A variation of the plain weave is the rib weave, which is used in such fabrics as broadcloth, poplin, faille, and grossgrain. Many rib-weave fabrics are made by inserting heavy filling yarns when weaving.

Another plain-weave variation is the basket weave. Its construction is not as firm as that of the plain or rib weaves, but it is attractive. Oxford cloth, a basket weave, is frequently used for men's and women's shirts. Monk's cloth is another example. One problem with this weave is a tendency toward yarn slippage: because it is somewhat loosely woven, thin yarns tend to slip and pack together where they should not. Basket-weave fabrics are good for coats, suits, and shirts.

The second basic weave pattern used in producing fabrics is the twill weave, identifiable by the diagonal line on the front of the fabric. Twill weave fabrics are strong, durable, and abrasion and wrinkle resistant. Twill weaves tend to show soil less than plain weaves, and maintenance is relatively easy. Some examples of twill weave fabrics include denim, gabardine, herringbone, wool broadcloth, cavalry twill, flannel, serge, surah, wool sharkskin, twill, and some wool tweeds. Twills are especially attractive for suits, skirts, and pants because of their wrinkle recovery and durability.

The third basic weave is the satin weave. Satin fabrics are chosen most often for their attractive appearance and sheen. They are not as durable as twill or plain fabrics, and they do tend to snag easily, but with their smooth surfaces they are ideal for lining coats and suits. Satin weave fabrics include slipper satin, satin-back crepe, bridal satin, sateen, moleskin crepe-back satin, and antique satin.

Knits

Knits are still as popular as ever, and no wonder. They are ideal for traveling and summer wear. Unlike woven fabrics, knits are created by the formation of loops, giving them some unique structural advantages.

- They have excellent elongation and elastic recovery properties, making them crush-resistant and practically wrinkle-free.
- They are porous and allow free circulation, making them ideal for warm climates.
- They allow for freedom of movement without permanent deformation of the fabric.
- They are lightweight and soft and require little ironing.

Knits should be treated with caution. Most can be machine washed and dried; however, wool knits such as cashmere sweaters must be dry-cleaned or hand-laundered. Be sure to read attached care labels.

There are two basic kinds of knits: warp knits and weft, or filling, knits. Warp knits include tricot milanese and raschel knits. In warp knits loops are formed in vertical directions.

Tricot, commonly used for lingerie, is soft, wrinkle-resistant, drapeable, run-resistant, and elastic. Because it is also strong and durable, it is often used in running and other athletic wear.

Raschel knits are usually open-structured and patterned. They are commonly seen in swimwear, curtains, window coverings, and modern laces work.

Milanese knits are similar to tricot knits; however, the machinery used to construct them is capable of forming elaborate patterns. These knits are not as durable as tricot and may tear easily.

Filling, or weft, knits include the ever-popular jersey fabrics. Double knits, rib, purl, and knitted pile fabrics are also filling knits. Such knits are made on a circular knitting frame with loops formed in the horizontal direction.

To tell the difference between weft and warp knits, look on the back side of the fabric. You will be able to see whether the loops go in a horizontal or vertical direction—except in the case of purl knits, which look the same front and back.

Jersey knits are used to make hosiery, sweaters, sportswear, T-shirts, and more. Although popular, a major disadvantage to these knits is their tendency to run once the yarn is broken.

Rib knits are created to give stretch with elastic fabrics. They are often seen on the wrists and lower edges of sweaters. They are warm, have good moisture absorption, are dimensionally stable, and do not ravel or curl when cut.

Double knits have excellent dimensional stability and are resistant to runs. They are easy to cut and sew and require minimal seam finishing. Double knits are resilient and also heavier and less elastic than single knits. Most double knits are constructed using the interlock stitch, and the surface is often rib-like in appearance. Extensive decorative patterns can be achieved with double knits.

Knitted pile fabrics are constructed on the double-knit technique. Many of the imitation furs on the market today are knitted pile fabrics.

Knits come in many forms to meet the demands of consumers' busy lifestyles. Comfortable and easy to care for, they are your number-one choice for travel and leisure.

Cotton Sweater Care

One of the most comfortable items in today's fashion is the cotton sweater. Cotton, one of the most comfortable fibers around, is coupled with the stretch of knit construction, with uniquely pleasing results.

Almost every designer offers at least one cotton sweater, and retail giants like Dillards, Nordstroms, and J.C. Penney stock them at moderate to better prices. Cotton sweaters can be machine washed and tumbled dry, but some of the finer ones require extra care. Here are some tips.

- Don't wash your sweater any more than you have to. Excessive cleaning, whether wet or dry, weakens the fibers.
- Stick to one cleaning process or another—don't switch. If you have been hand-washing continue to do so. If you dry-clean, always dry-clean.
- When hand washing, use mild detergents and tepid water. When using hand-washing detergents such as Woolite, be sure to follow the

directions explicitly. These detergents, although mild, can damage your sweater if directions are ignored.

- When drying your sweater, roll it in a clean towel, then lay it flat on a dry towel—on top of the dryer, perhaps. Be sure you wash your sweater on a dry day.
- Should you choose to machine dry to shape a stretched sweater, turn the sweater inside out before doing so. The dryer can damage the surface fibers as the sweater is tossed around.
- Do not hang up your sweaters; fold them or roll them up and keep them in a drawer or on a shelf.
- Cotton has a tendency to pill when met with friction. To alleviate this, try brushing your sweaters with a lint brush when you begin to notice tiny balls, or pills, on the surface. This will help keep your sweaters looking great for years to come.

Care of Shoes and Other Leather Goods

Shoe care is simple but extremely important. While the price of leather has soared, the quality of shoes has gone down. Shoes don't last years; if they are not cared for, they won't last even one year. The key to keeping your shoes and other leather goods in tip-top condition is polish. Polish protects the leather from drying out or being ruined by a sudden rain. Avoid quick-drying liquid polishes: these contain alcohol, which can dry out the leather. Instead, use cream polishes such as Meltonian, which cleans and shines shoes in one step.

When you purchase new shoes, a new bag, or a new briefcase, treat the item to a paste-polish rubdown to ward off soil penetration. After each wearing, brush shoes and give them at least a day's rest. This allows them to air out and foot perspiration to dry. While shoes are at rest, preserve their shape with shoe trees. When you travel, place shoes in bags to protect them and your clothing.

If you do get caught in the rain, let your shoes dry naturally away from any direct heat source, such as a radiator. Stuff the toe area with some paper towels to absorb moisture and to help retain the shape of the shoe. Remove any salt or stains with white vinegar and water mixed in equal parts. Once the shoes have dried, condition and polish them.

Check shoe heels and soles periodically. Are the heels worn through? Send them to a repair shop immediately. Or perhaps the heel of your shoe gets caught on something and the leather tears. Send them to the repair shop. Don't wait until they're ready to be thrown away to get them repaired. At the price of shoes today, proper care is essential.

Understanding Care Instructions

The law mandates that care instructions be attached to all apparel, and, indeed, the care instructions specified by manufacturers are the safest way to clean your garments. This is all well and good, but what do these instructions mean? First, some basic rules. If temperature is not mentioned, then any temperature may be used. If bleach is not mentioned, then any bleach may be used. And if ironing instructions are not mentioned, that means the fabric is treated or constructed in such a way that ironing is unnecessary. The chart on the following pages will aid you in decoding care instructions.

What Care Instructions Mean*

Washing Machine Methods

Machine Wash
Use automatic washer.

Warm
Initial water temperature setting 90°F to 110°F (32°C to 43°C) — comfortable to hands.

Cold
Initial water temperature setting same as cold tap water up to 85°F (29°C)

Do Not Have Commercially Laundered
Do not employ a laundry that uses special formulations, sour rinses, or extremely high temperatures, or that is employed for commercial, industrial, or institutional purposes.

Small Load
Smaller than normal wash load.

Delicate Cycle or Gentle Cycle
Set washer to gentle cycle with slow agitation and reduced time.

Durable Press Cycle or Permanent Press Cycle
Cool-down rinse or cold rinse before spinning.

Separately
Alone.

With Like Colors
With garments that are similar in color and brightness.

Wash Inside Out
Turn the garment inside out to protect the surface of the fabric.

Warm Rinse
Initial water temperature setting 90°F to 110°F (32°C to 43°C).

Cold Rinse
Initial water temperature setting should be like cold tap water.

Rinse Thoroughly
Rinse several times to remove soap, bleach, or detergent.

No Spin or Do Not Spin
Remove material at the start of the final spin cycle.

No Wring or Do Not Wring
Do not wring by hand and do not use a roller wringer.

Washing by Hand

Hand Wash
Use water, detergent, or soap and gently squeeze the garment several times.

Warm
Initial water temperature 90°F to 110°F (32°C to 43°C) (comfortable to hands)

Cold
Initial water temperature should be the same as cold tap water.

Separately
Alone.

With Like Colors
With garments of the same color and brightness.

No Wring or Twist
Do not twist the garment. Handle it so as not to distort or wrinkle the garment.

Damp Wipe Only
Clean fabric surface with a damp cloth or sponge.

Drying

Tumble Dry
Use machine dryer.

Medium
Use medium heat setting.

Low
Use low heat setting.

Durable Press or Permanent Press
Use permanent press setting.
No Heat
Set dryer to operate without heat.

Remove Promptly
When items are dry remove them from the dryer to avoid wrinkling.

Drip Dry
Air dry, without wringing or shaping, on a plastic or padded hanger.

Line Dry
Hang outside on a line or inside on a line or bar.

Ironing and Pressing

Iron
Ironing is needed. Any temperature is safe.

Warm Iron
Set iron at medium temperature.

Cool Iron
Set iron at lowest temperature.

Do Not Iron
For garments that do not need to be smoothed or finished with an iron.

No Steam or Do Not Steam
Refrain from using steam when ironing.

Iron Wrong Side Only
Turn item inside out when ironing.

Steam Only
Steam with steamer or iron with steam but no contact pressure.

Steam Press or Steam Iron
Use iron at steam setting.
Iron Damp
Dry garments should be moistened prior to ironing.

Use Press Cloth
Use a dry iron or a damp cloth between the iron and the garment when ironing.

Bleaching

Bleach When Needed
Any bleach can be used when necessary.

No Bleach or Do Not Bleach
Self-explanatory.

Only Non-Chlorine Bleach When Needed
Self-explanatory.

Washing or Dry-cleaning

Wash or Dry-clean, Any Normal Method
Can be machine washed, dried, and ironed at any temperature. Any bleach can be used. Garment can be dry-cleaned using any kind of solvent.

Dry-clean
Can be dry-cleaned at professional or self-service dry-cleaners. Involves a process in which soil is removed by organic solvents in a machine.

Professionally Dry-clean
Use a professional dry-cleaner; avoid self-service dry-cleaners.

* This care guide courtesy of the Consumer Affairs Committee, American Apparel Manufacturers Association, and based on the Voluntary Guide of the Textile Industry Advisory Committee for Consumer Interest.

Selected Bibliography

Adler, Mortimer J. (1983). *How to Speak How to Listen*, New York: Macmillan Publishing Company

Baldridge, Letitia (1985). *Complete Guide to Executive Manners*, Rawson Associates, New York: Macmillan Publishing Company

Buckley, Hilda M. and Roach, M.E. (1974), "Clothing as a Nonverbal Communication of Social and Political Attitudes," *Home Economics Research Journal*, 3(2): 94-102.

Fast, Julius (1970). *Body Language*, New York: M. Evans and Company, Inc.

Hall, Edward T. (1963). "Proxemics: A Study of Man's Spatial Relationship." *Man's Image in Medicine and Anthropology*. New York: International Press, 442-445.

Heslin, Richard cited in Knapp, Mark (1980), *Essentials of Nonverbal Communication*, New York: Holt, Rinehart & Winston, 152-155.

Jackson, Carole (1984). *Color Me Beautiful*, New York: Ballentine Books.

Joseph, Marjory L. (1984). *Essentials of Textiles*, New York: Holt, Rinehart and Winston.

Kaiser, Susan B. (1985). *The Social Psychology of Clothing and Personal Adornment*, New York: Macmillan Publishing Company.

McGill, Leonard (1983). *Stylewise*, New York: G. P. Putnam's Sons.

Molloy, John T. (1988). *The New Dress for Success*, New York: Warner Books.

Molloy, John T. (1977). *The Woman's Dress For Success Book*, New York: Warner Books.

Morrisey, George L. and Schrest, Thomas L. (1987*). Effective Business and Technical Presentations* (3rd edition), Reading, Massachusetts: Addison-Wesley Publishing Company, Inc.

Munter, Mary (1987). *Business Communication: Strategy and Skill*, Englewood Cliffs, New Jersey: Prentice Hall, Inc.

Pease, Allan (1981). *Signals*, New York: Bantam Books.

Post, Elizabeth L. (1984). *Etiquette: A Guide to Modern Manners* (14th edition), New York: Harper & Row, Publishers.

Seitz, Victoria A. (1990). *Power Dressing*, Denton, TX: RonJon Publishing.

Waggoner, Glen and Moloney, Kathleen (1987). *Esquire Etiquette*, New York: Macmillan Publishing Company.

Zunin, Leonard, M.D. and Zunin, Natalie (1972). *Contact: The First Four Minutes*, New York: Ballantine Books.

Final Notes

A couple of notes are necessary to give this book the finishing touch. I think it's important to realize that even though we have talked about etiquette, body language, and dress, other areas must also be addressed that complete the total picture. One of those areas is health. Taking care of yourself through preventive care, eating properly, having enough sleep, and handling stress is part of the frosting on the cake. In essence, when you take care of your insides it reflects on your outsides. Guaranteed, I speak from experience. If you let your health go and don't take care of yourself, people can see it in your eyes, hair, body, and productivity at work.

Fitness is also critical to topping off a great look. It's not a matter of whether you're proportioned or not, it's whether your body is toned. Besides, exercise is great for handling stress, giving you more energy and more years to your life. I really believe what some experts feel exercise is — the real "fountain of youth." Sometimes I would look around at other people my age and say "hey, I'm well preserved!" Even if you're older don't give up. I thought it was funny what an acquaintance said, "If I knew I was going to live this long I would have taken better care of myself!" Start now. Exercise and be fit, even if your not a "he man" or blessed with a model's figure, being fit really makes a big difference with the level of confidence you have in yourself. Besides when you're fit, your clothes look better on you.

The third point that is critical to your image is the blessing of a good education. You don't need graduate school but you do need to be well versed in reading, writing, and speaking the English language. One of the major complaints I hear from executives is that people entering or currently in the job market cannot communicate orally or via the written word. Don't hold back learning these critical skills because of ridicule from your peers. You are leap years ahead if you can acknowledge your weaknesses and attempt to change them. Remember life is a learning process. The day you stop learning is the day you die. All in all, a person that claims that he or she knows it all and is not willing to continue learning is boring.

The fourth point I'd like to make is to enjoy life. Some of us enjoy working. I am one of those people but it's taken time, great friends, and a niece, to help me learn to take time to enjoy life and the people closest to me. I have to admit, when I wrote this book I was pretty engrossed in it. You only go around once in life. In essence, you are born and you die, what you do on your journey in between is up to you. None of us get out of here alive, so enjoy the experiences and people you encounter on your journey. Learn as much as you can from others and your experiences — enjoy. Much success to you!

Index

FIND MORE ON THIS TOPIC BY VISITING
BusinessTown.com
The Web's big site for growing businesses!

- ☑ **Separate channels on all aspects of starting and running a business**
- ☑ **Lots of info on how to do business online**
- ☑ **1,000+ pages of savvy business advice**
- ☑ **Complete web guide to thousands of useful business sites**
- ☑ **Free e-mail newsletter**
- ☑ **Question and answer forums, and more!**

Accounting
Basic, Credit & Collections, Projections, Purchasing/Cost Control

Advertising
Magazine, Newspaper, Radio, Television, Yellow Pages

Business Opportunities
Ideas for New Businesses, Business for Sale, Franchises

Business Plans
Creating Plans & Business Strategies

Finance
Getting Money, Money Problem Solutie

Letters & Forms
Looking Professional, Sample Letters & Forms

Getting Started
Incorporating, Choosing a Legal Struc

Hiring & Firing
Finding the Right People, Legal Issues

Home Business
Home Business Ideas, Getting Started

Internet
Getting Online, Put Your Catalog on the Web

Legal Issues
Contracts, Copyrights, Patents, Trademarks

Managing a Small Business
Growth, Boosting Profits, Mistakes to Avoid, Competing with the Giants

Managing People
Communications, Compensation, Motivation, Reviews, Problem Employees

Marketing
Direct Mail, Marketing Plans, Strategie Publicity, Trade Shows

Office Setup
Leasing, Equipment, Supplies

Presentations
Know Your Audience, Good Impressio

Sales
Face to Face, Independent Reps, Telemarketing

Selling a Business
Finding Buyers, Setting a Price, Legal Issues

Taxes
Employee, Income, Sales, Property, Use

Time Management
Can You Really Manage Time?

Travel & Maps
Making Business Travel Fun

Valuing a Business
Simple Valuation Guidelines